POST-MODERN PILGRIMS

FIRST CENTURY PASSION
FOR THE 21ST CENTURY WORLD

POST-MODERN PILGRIMS

LEONARD SWEET

BROADMAN
&HOLMAN
PUBLISHERS

NASHVILLE, TENNESSEE

0–8054–2137–8

Published by Broadman & Holman Publishers, Nashville, Tennessee

Dewey Decimal Classification: 261
Subject Heading: CHRISTIANITY AND CULTURE

Biblical translations are cited with the following acronyms:
NEB: The New English Bible, © The Delegates of the Oxford University Press
and the Syndics of the Cambridge University Press, 1961, 1970, reprinted
by permission. NIV: The Holy Bible, New International Version, copyright
© 1973, 1978, 1984 by International Bible Society. NJB: Excerpts from
The New Jerusalem Bible, copyright © 1984 by Darton, Longman
and Todd, Ltd and Doubleday and Company, Inc. Used by permission
of the publisher. NKJV: New King James Version, copyright © 1979,
1980, 1982, Thomas Nelson, Inc., Publishers. NRSV: New Revised Standard
Version of the Bible, copyright © 1989 by the Division of Christian
Education of the National Council of Churches of Christ in the United
States of America, used by permission, all rights reserved. REB: The Revised
English Bible, © Oxford University Press and Cambridge University
Press, 1989. RSV: Revised Standard Version of the Bible, copyrighted
1946, 1952, © 1971, 1973. TLB: The Living Bible, copyright © Tyndale
House Publishers, Wheaton, Ill., 1971, used by permission.

Library of Congress Cataloging-in-Publication Data

Sweet, Leonard I.
    Postmodern pilgrims : first century passion for the 21st century world /
Leonard Sweet.
        p. cm.
    Includes bibliographical references.
    ISBN 0–8054–2137–8 (hb)
    1. Christianity and culture. 2. Postmodernism—Religious aspects—
Christianity. 3. Civilization, Modern—1950 I. Title.

BR115.C8 S94 2000
261—dc21
                                                                00–037881
                        1 2 3 4 5 04 03 02 01 00

To Betty O'Brien

My personal Santa Lucia

Contents

Acknowledgments

Writing itself is an act of faith, and nothing else.
—E. B. White

The above motto of the National Book Foundation was adopted from E. B. White, who himself won the medal in 1971. It expresses the sentiments of every author who dares the alchemy of turning thoughts into things.

But the "faith" involved in writing a book is as much others' "faith" in you as your own "faith" in the creative process. Anna Claire Mauerhan, Phillip Connolly, Lyn Caterson, and Aana Lisa Whatley believed in me enough to stand by and struggle on through my thick dreams, thin means, and sticky ends. There is an old Appalachian saying: "In a strong wind, even turkeys can fly." The strong gusts lifted even this stout bird aloft. Thom and Joani Schultz of Group Publishing had enough faith in my musings about EPIC models of ministry to encourage a preliminary sketching out of what a book like this would look like ("A New Reformation: Re-creating Worship for a Postmodern World," in *Experience God in Worship*, ed. George Barna [Loveland, Colo.: Group Publishing, 1999]).

There are no solitary authors: the essence of publishing is not solo. My editor Len Goss taught me the foolishness of leading with your chin. Steve Kriss made sure I was aware of various "wet cement" moments in the casting of this book. Rob Duncan is more than a magician/mentor/technician/ administrator. He's a friend and confidante who helps me, as one of our students puts it, "doubleclick to Holy Spirit" (Ned Buckner). I apologize to Peter Sheldrup for stealing the title of his video *Postmodern Pilgrims*. But I've been a walking ad for this video resource for so long and recommended it to so many people that I'm entitled. One more time: to order his excellent resource, send a $20 check to Peter Sheldrup, 2804 Williams Street, Bellingham, WA 98225. The worship center in early Christianity was the dining table. Nobody presides better at "the Table" in my academic house than colleague/confederate/confidante Ginny Samuel Cetuk.

A constant background in my ministry is more than my executive assistant's "percussive maintenance" on her computer. It's Lyn Stuntebeck's unyielding devotion to "The Mission." The philosopher Ludwig Wittgenstein, whom I discovered in the course of writing this book, wrote that "it is so difficult to find the beginning. Or, better: it is difficult to begin at the beginning. And not try to go further back" *(On Certainty,* ed. G. E. M. Anscombe and G. H. Von Wright; trans. Denis Paul and G. E. M. Anscombe [New York: Harper, 1972], 62e). Every one of us needs people who can help us find the beginning and begin there. My wife Elizabeth Rennie does that for me—and in so doing enables me to inhabit a habitable cosmos and hospitable climate for writing.

If readers begin to hear the ice crack the farther an author skates from areas of expertise, Betty O'Brien is the best icemaker any author could wish. She opens up fire hydrants every day to make sure my brash skates don't dig through the cracks. Betty is more than a research assistant. She's my friend, my intellectual guardian angel, and my court of last resort. Her faith authorized me to write a book like *Postmodern Pilgrims*. I dedicate it to her.

Leonard Sweet

Orcas Island 1/1/2000

FOREWORD

The Twentieth Century is the name of a train that no longer runs."

—David Lehman[1]

Between 1947 and 1949, a conservative Christian philosopher and theologian delivered a set of lectures at the universities of Tübingen and Munich at which he broadcast a "crisis": the end of the world. "Today the modern age is essentially over." The church was on the right track, he argued, but riding the wrong train.

These lectures are as relevant today as when they were first delivered. Entitled *The End of the Modern World*, their author Monsignor Romano Guardini (1885–1968), sought "to apprehend the nature of the world epoch which is being born out of the womb of history," a history which yet "has not named its offspring."[2]

> The chains of cause and effect that it established will of course continue to hold. Historical epochs are not neatly severed like the steps of a laboratory experiment. While one era prevails, its successor is already forming, and its predecessor continues to exert influence for a long time. To this day we find elements of a still-vital antiquity in southern Europe, and we run across strong medieval currents in many places. Thus in the yet nameless epoch which we feel breaking in on us from all sides, the last consequences of the modern age are still being drawn, although that which

xiii

determined the essence of that age no longer determines the character of the historical epoch now beginning.[3]

What Guardini saw as the three historical ages of Western history (classical, medieval, and modern) were bound together by remarkable continuities. The "historical epoch" that now lies before us is so new, Guardini argued, that Christians cannot either "go back" or "go forward." We can only make a fresh start, a new beginning. Given our "radical discontinuity" with the past, we must restate Christian faith in a manner that takes full account of an anti-Christian, Einsteinian universe.

This book you are holding in your hands goes halfway with Guardini. He's right about this: It *is* a whole new world out there. More and more are admitting it. Of the five coping mechanisms for relating to any transition ("hold out," "keep out," "move out," "close out," "reach out"),[4] fewer and fewer are able to "hold out" and deny the changes that are taking place.

A poll of business executives found an astonishing 49 percent taking the most radical position they could take about the future: we are living in revolutionary times and are at the very beginnings of an entirely new economic era that requires a fundamental reinvention of how we live, work, and play.[5] The most respected corporate executive in the world today, General Electric's Jack Welch, corresponds with his team under the signature of "dyb.com," short for "destroyyourbusiness.com." In a 1999 *New York Times* interview, Michael Armstrong said of AT&T's new cable venture: "We need to figure out how to build it, how to deploy it, how to support it, how to maintain it." I challenge you to come up with a better definition of a start-up than this by the chair and CEO of AT&T.

In October 1999, the Dow dropped from its index Texaco, Sears Roebuck, Union Carbide, Chevron, and Goodyear. It put in their place some technology companies and recent start-ups: Microsoft, Intel, SBC Communications, Hewlett-Packard, and Home Depot. We are all poised at the beginning of something very new—a start-up culture which (for want of any better designation) is being referred to as "postmodern."

✝ ✝ ✝

"The challenge for the Net is to create new models for the new world, as opposed to porting over old models. We take things from the physical world and put them on the Internet and then wonder why there's no profit in it; of course, there's no profit in it! Shame on you."

—Jay S. Walker, founder, Priceline.com[6]

✝ ✝ ✝

There may be fewer and fewer "holdouts" to such a view. But the numbers are increasing of "keep outs" (hunker in the bunker), "move outs" (relocate and hide in nostalgic yearning for the status quo ante), and "closeouts" (toss in the towel and admit defeat).

This book you are holding joins Guardini in a "reach out" strategy that responds creatively to the new world. But this book departs with Guardini over how Christians are to "reach out" and enter this new world. Guardini contends that Christians are unable to move either forward or backward. *Postmodern Pilgrims* "reaches out" for a back-to-the-future methodology of movement that is simultaneously backward and forward.[7]

The essence of an ancientfuture mode of locating the Christian faith in this new world is what I have called and developed elsewhere as the "double ring."[8] British evangelical theologian John R. W. Stott calls it "double listening"[9]— one ear listening to God's Word and the other to God's World. According to Stott, "double listening" is

> the faculty of listening to two voices at the same time, the voice of God through Scripture and the voices of men and women around us. These voices will often contradict one another, but our purpose in listening to them both is to discover how they relate to each other. Double listening is indispensable to Christian discipleship and Christian mission.[10]

The greatest symbol for the inherent "doubleness" of the Christian faith is the cross: the intersection of the horizontal and the vertical, the overlap of the divine on the human, the interface of the ancient and the future.

A cross Christianity, a faith that is both ancient and future, both historical and contemporary, is what is outlined in this book. *Postmodern Pilgrims* is an attempt to show the church how to camp in the future in the light of the past. It argues that the Bible outlines a double procession of rejection and affirmation in terms of culture: a movement away from the world to God is followed by a movement back to the world as we love what God loves and do what Jesus did. Unless we can hear God's voice calling to us from out of the whirlwind, can we hear that same voice calling to us from within the whirlwind?

In fact, *Postmodern Pilgrims* argues that ministry in the twenty-first century has more in common with the first century than with the modern world that is collapsing all around us. *Postmodern Pilgrims* aims to demodernize the Christian consciousness and reshape its way of life according to a more biblical vision of life that is dawning with the coming of the postmodern era. Hence the subtitle: *First Century Passion for the 21st Century World.*

Christians should not embrace a postmodern worldview; we must not adapt to postmodernity. Jesus is "the same yesterday, today, and forever" (Heb. 13:8 NKJV). In other words, Jesus is the same in three time zones and two dimensions: the timely (past and present) and the timeless (forever). But we do need to incarnate the timeless in the timely. Postmoderns do need to probe the living-out of our faith in light of the classical Christian tradition.

The ancient ways are more relevant than ever. The mystery of how ancient words can have spiritual significance in this new world is evident in the cultural quest for "soul" and "spirit." The very talk of soul and spirit is the talk of a very ancient language, a first-century language largely abandoned by the modern world but a language more fitting today than ever.

The "double-ring" or "double-listening" method is elaborated in Acts 8:32–33. After Jesus' crucifixion, Philip and the Ethiopian are traveling on the desert road from Jerusalem to Gaza. The Ethiopian read aloud what was to him a perplexing passage from Isaiah (Isa. 53:7–8). Starting from where he was, Philip "proceeded to explain the Good News of Jesus to him" (Acts 8:35). In other words, the Ethiopian was confused, disturbed, and searching. Philip believed in the interpretive power of the gospel to help us understand all of life. By bringing into convergence one eye focused on the Word of God and the other eye focused on the implications of that Word on the world God made, the Ethiopian's life was transformed, and he became a "new person."

† † †

The earlier culture will become a heap of rubble and finally a heap of ashes, but spirits will hover over the ashes.

—Ludwig Wittgenstein[11]

† † †

Postmodern Pilgrims reads what is going on in the world in the light of the Bible. It attempts to exegete today's culture by the light shed from the cross and to understand all of life in the light of the Christian tradition. Movement into the future is based on the dynamic interplay of contraries (preservation and transcendence) that are less binary opposites than complementary forces that fuse together to form a superior synthesis. In the words of philosopher Peter Marshall:

> In logical terms, thesis and antithesis may be subsumed into a higher synthesis which contains them both. In biological terms, father and mother may be said to be united in their children. . . . Without the interpenetration of opposites and their resolution, the world would remain in a static condition of rigid immobility.[12]

In short, in an ancientfuture methodology of movement, the affirmation of the past can become an acceptance of the future.

Postmodern culture is not the first crisis culture, to be sure. Culture and crisis go together like A&W, A&P, Abercrombe & Fitch. Everyone knows what *crisis* stands for in Chinese characters: danger and opportunity. Even better is what *crisis* stands for in Hebrew: *mash-ber*, a word also used for birth stool, a seat upon which a woman in ancient times sat as she gave birth.

If ever there were a moment for birth-stool creativity, it is now. Of all the leadership arts,[13] creativity and imagination are some of the most "in crisis" in the church. Humans live in the imagination. Without imagination, all hearts are closed, all desires unknown. Like a spider spins from within the web, so we spin from our imaginations the worlds we inhabit.

The history of civilizations is the history of the human imagination.

Unfortunately, the postmodern imagination is proving more creative at faking reality than at fixing reality. Our best minds today are obsessed with helping us escape more than engage our multiple "crises." Compare the state of DisneyWorld's Main Street USA with the condition of USAmerica's small-town main streets. Compare what you can do at the cybergames *Age of Empires II* (Microsoft) and *SimCity* with what we're doing at Harlem, Watts, and other similar cities. We consume in our real lives (even our church life), and we create in our cyber life.

A case in point is the megahit television special *Who Wants to Be a Millionaire?*[14] Unlike any other game show in history, here is a program that draws from all demographic groups. When most game-show watchers are over fifty-five, the viewers of *Who Wants to Be a Millionaire?* virtually mirror the U.S. population. College students turned its show times into campuswide parties. Even the narrow band of diversity in its contestants does not prohibit a widespread diversity of viewers.

What is the secret of its success? What do the show's producers know about how to reach postmoderns from which we in the church might learn?

First, *Who Wants to Be a Millionaire?* is less a game show than an experience. Through music, lights, suspense, symbols, and fast-paced narratives, viewers are summoned into a shared experience with both contestants and other viewers.

Second, *Who Wants to Be a Millionaire?* is built on a participatory—not a representative—model. "Lifelines" enable the studio audience and the cyber audience to become part of the "experience" itself. By inviting the contestants to call on friends, family, and the audience for help, there is a blurring of the lines between viewers and contestants.

Third, *Who Wants to Be a Millionaire?* is image-based. The image of a million dollars and what it means to be a millionaire is well established in postmodern culture. Add to the millionaire image the everyman image of the contestant, with questions easy enough for everyone to answer, and the question mark at the end of the show's title begs entrance into every heart. Here is a game show built not on who is the smartest but on you're-smart-enough-to-be-sitting-here assurances if only you had the luck of the draw.

Fourth, *Who Wants to Be a Millionaire?* positions a lone individual at the center of the stage but surrounded physically by an audience rooting for him (some of whom are carefully spotlighted as friends and family) and surrounded virtually by a community of twenty-three million plus cheerleaders, some of whom contestants can connect with at any minute if they get in over their heads and need help. In other words, the success of *Who Wants to Be a Millionaire?* is that, unlike other game shows, it has successfully transitioned from rational to experiential, from representative to participatory, from word-based to image-driven, and from individual to connecting the individual and the communal.

Through a process of "double listening," *Postmodern Pilgrims* introduces an EPIC model of doing church that is biblically absolute but culturally relative: Experiential, Participatory, Image-driven, Connected. Like the church of the first century, the twenty-first-century church must learn to measure success not by its budgets and buildings but by its creativity and imagination. Like the church of the first century, the twenty-first-century church must measure success not by the size of bank accounts or biceps but by the strength of brains and birth stools. In the midst of a consumer culture that is built on earnings, yearnings, and bottom lines, the church must be a conceiving culture that is built on God's grace where the "top things" and "top of the lines" in life are given freely, tended and tilled conservatively, and distributed liberally. If conception doesn't replace consumption as the primary GNP in the church first, it never will in the wider culture.

✝ ✝ ✝

*Those who have lived well for their own time have
lived well for all times.*

—Ancient proverb

✝ ✝ ✝

The challenge for Postmodern Pilgrims is to give post-modern culture a "witness": to "do church" in ways that measure success by conceivings rather than consumings. Any church that says and does otherwise is a product of "this present evil age" (Gal.1:4 KJV) and not Christ's gospel.

The crisis of evangelism in a postmodern world is this:

- In a culture of Bible-believing churches filled with people who don't read the Bible . . .
- In a culture of soul-saving churches filled with people who never get personally involved in soul-saving[15] . . .
- In a culture where the last five U.S. presidents (Gerald Ford, Jimmy Carter, Ronald Reagan, George Bush, and Bill Clinton) all described themselves as "born again Christians" . . .
- In a culture where consumerism is the number one religion . . .
- In a culture where Deepak Chopra, Oprah Winfrey, and Larry Dossey are more authoritative voices than Moses, Jesus, or even Mohammed . . .
- In a culture where the Bible no longer provides the spectacles through which people gaze . . .

✝   How do you lift up the Messiah's message of the cross in the midst of this Mars Hill culture?

† How do you present the "old rugged cross" as the most powerful symbol for understanding life and transforming lives?

† How do you convey the belief that what Jesus says is more relevant to people's lives and our post-modern crises than all our philosophers and scientists combined?

† How do you hand people the Bible and tell them what they are getting: the black book of living, the essential text for solving every crisis out there?

† How do you convey the truth that the true "experts" on what is going on in the world today are Matthew, Mark, Luke, John, and that this Bible is the text for solving whatever crisis slaps us in the face?

† How do you hand postmoderns a Bible and say to them, "Here's a book that is custom designed by the Holy Spirit for you. This book has your name written on it and all over it."

† How do you persuade postmoderns that the Gospels contain an anthropology of religion that has never been surpassed by anything the social sciences have ever come up with? Or as Dallas Willard puts it, how do you convince postmodern professionals "that Jesus is the smartest person in their field"— whether that field be psychology, biology, immunology or theology?

† † †

Introduction

Kiss and Tell

My favorite actor growing up was Kirk Douglas. He starred in the first movie I ever saw, *Spartacus* (1959). I had to sneak out to see it because movies were forbidden when I was growing up. My favorite Kirk Douglas movie was the sci-fi film *Saturn 3* with the screenplay by Martin Amis. Now in his mid-eighties, with almost the same number of films to his credit, actor Douglas has become writer Douglas, with a children's novella and two autobiographies already to his credit.[1]

In one of his books Douglas tells of his lifelong resolve to pick up hitchhikers whenever it was feasible. One afternoon he picked up a sailor on leave. After jumping into the car and throwing his backpack into the backseat, the sailor did a double take, then a triple take, and then blurted out to Douglas, "Hey, man, do you know *who* you are?"

There are two fundamental questions in life. "Do you know who you are?" is perhaps the most fundamental question anyone can ask. And answer. My answer is basic but complex. It comes first from Isaiah 43:4 ("You are precious and honored in my sight, and . . . I love you" NIV),

1

and then from Jesus ("As the Father has loved me, so I have loved you" John 15:9 NIV). I'm the one Jesus loves.

✝ ✝ ✝

You are worse off than you ever dared to imagine,
but God loves you more than you ever dared to hope.
—Manhattan church planter Tim Keller

✝ ✝ ✝

The second question is like unto the first, except for one word's difference. From the Gulf War of 1990–91 comes the story of three British soldiers, stumbling in the desert. Separated from their troops in the fighting, they were lost, hungry, and searching for help when they literally bumped into a four-star USAmerican general.

Excitedly they blurted out, "Do you know where we are?"

The general stiffened. Upset at their lack of protocol and rituals of respect, he looked down at them and demanded, "Do you know who I am?"

One of the English soldiers elbowed his buddy and mumbled, "Now we're in deep trouble. We don't know where we are, and he doesn't know who he is."

Do you know *where* you are, church?

✝ ✝ ✝

The institutional church in the next twenty years will
continue more and more to look like the pink Cadillac
with the huge tail fins.

—Anonymous quote

† † †

Perhaps three romance stories can help us answer this second question.

Romance Story 1

Two high school sophomores had been dating for some time. As they walked up the steps of her porch, which was lit by moonlight, the guy decided to make his move.

"Can I kiss you goodnight?"

His date looked up at him adoringly, gave him a big, bright smile, and said nothing. Not knowing how to interpret the silence, his mind raced for a minute until it hit on what was wrong: bad grammar. So he tried again.

"May I kiss you goodnight?"

Once again, the gal dazzled him with her smile, titled her head upward, and closed her eyes. But she still said nothing.

Totally flustered, the guy blurted out, "Are you deaf?"

She opened her eyes and spoke for the first time: "Are you paralyzed?"

Are you paralyzed, church?

Why can't we kiss it?

Why can't we kiss this culture?

Why can't we help this culture itself kiss?

Why are we more prone to send this postmodern culture hate mail than love letters? Why can't we teach this culture the best definition of God that has ever been written? "Whoever does not love does not know God, because God is love" (1 John 4:8 NIV).

✝ ✝ ✝

Mercy and truth have met. . . .
Justice and peace have kissed!

—Psalm 85:10 TLB

✝ ✝ ✝

ROMANCE STORY 2

Charley and Sara sometimes hang out together, but Charley really doesn't like Sara very much. One day it hits him:

> The way to help Sara is to date her! If we were to go out, my strengths could rub off on her, and she would be far better off for it. It will require sacrifice on my part, but it's the least I can do.

> Charley marches up to Sara's door with a book entitled *100 Things Sara Needs to Change in Order to Become a Real Person.* He rings the doorbell. When she answers, he shoves the book in her face and states, "I've decided it would be best for you if we date. When you finish reading this, I'll be waiting in my truck!"

Charley is Gene Greitenbach's metaphor for the current state of most evangelism in USAmerica.[2]

✝ ✝ ✝

At what else does that touching of lips aim but at a junction of souls?

Philosopher Favorinus of Arles[3]

✝ ✝ ✝

ROMANCE STORY 3

A cartoon in the *Wall Street Journal* shows a man listening to an answering-machine message: "Hi! This is your wife. To find out what's for dinner, press 1. To apologize for something you said, press 2. To say 'I love you,' press 3."

People are waiting for someone to press 3. Will the church press 3 to communicate with this culture?

Do you remember one of the earliest songs you learned on the playground? Your buddies sang it to you when they found out you liked someone:

Lenny and Linda
Sitting in a tree
K-I-S-S-I-N-G

A lot of people out there are trying to kiss postmodern culture, even if the church isn't.

For three decades a rock group called KISS has mesmerized our kids. From the late 1970s, when KISS was the most popular band in the world, to today, with their 1998 release *Psycho Circus*, these monsters of rock have been KISSing us not just with music, but with rugs, mouse pads, KISSmas balls, T-shirts, CD clocks, even limited-edition pewter figurines ($575).[4]

Aveda, the beauty legend, uses lipstick sales to promote "kiss'n'care" campaigns.

Candy companies have made fortunes by kissing us, and they don't care whether we're modern or postmodern. Hershey Foods' 1998 annual report asks, "Do you remember your first kiss?" and features stockholders ruminating about candies they've known and loved.

Expensive rhinestone kiss purses dangle from women's hips all over the world.

The coffee-bar Xando (as in "X" and "O") wants to kiss and hug you with their shocking "Mocha Kiss" (mocha with sherry, Irish cream, mandarin orange, and whipped cream).

A Dr. Pepper commercial features an assortment of people smacking you from the other side of the screen.

ANA Airways, "Japan's largest and most lovable airline," wants you to kiss it and features a big smacker on its nose cone.

Cole Porter wants us to beg, "Kiss Me, Kate."

Let's try a little experiment. Finish this sentence:
"Winston tastes good . . ."
". . . *like a cigarette should.*"
Now finish this sentence:
"Plop, Plop, Fizz, Fizz . . ."
". . . *Oh, what a relief it is.*"

The last time these commercials aired was more than twenty-five years ago. How did that message get burned into your brain?

Madison Avenue can so sear our skulls with messages about tobacco and antacids that we remember them for a quarter of a century. The church has the greatest message that ever was sent: You're the one Jesus loves! Why can't we imprint this culture with the good news of the gospel? Why can't we show the world that the love of Jesus Christ is the most powerful force in the universe? Why can't we kiss this postmodern culture?

"But we are kissing it," you say. "We have worship and church school on Sunday, and youth group on Sunday night, and Bible study on Monday, and prayer groups all week long." Sometimes a kiss is not a kiss. A peck on the cheek is not a kiss. "Playing church" (meet-eat-and-beat-it churches) is not a kiss. You kiss someone with your eyes, with your smiles, with your language, with your presence, with your music, with your timetables. A kiss can also be a kiss-off. Or a Mafia kiss of death. Or the devil's "kiss me where I have no nose."[5]

Ultimately, kissing is not something you do with your lips but with your life. The kind of kissing I'm talking about goes beyond lip service to life service.

Two women were walking down a New York street when they spotted a frog. The frog looked up and said, "I used to be a handsome, wealthy stockbroker. But I was turned into a frog. If one of you kisses me on the lips, I will be turned back to my original self."

One of the women stooped down, picked up the frog, and placed him in her pocket. The two friends walked on for a while, but the other finally got curious and said, "Aren't you going to kiss the frog on the lips and turn him back to what he was?"

"Nope," she replied, "I'd rather have a talking frog."

We'd rather have a talking frog than kiss this culture to wake up to the healing power of Jesus Christ. If anything, the church's message to this cyberculture is "kiss off." The culture of course returns the favor. And the two never meet. "The virtual absence of organized religion from Western public intellectual life," writes psychologist Merlin Donald, "is a drastic break with our past."[6]

Kiss is not simply a cute metaphor. Nor is kiss defined here as an erotic exercise. Many cultures are unfamiliar with mouth-to-mouth, mucous-membrane kissing, also known as the "labial kiss." It is not a universal cultural phenomenon and is totally unknown in some Asian cultures. In many places nose-rubbing is more popular than mouth-rubbing.

Sigmund Freud was not the first to wonder why kissing is so popular in the West since kissing does not use any part of the body's sexual apparatus but the body's digestive tract.[7]

† † †

We somehow think that the Church is here for us; we forget that we are the Church, and we're here for the world.
—Mosaic (Los Angeles) pastor Erwin McManus

† † †

When Christianity was more a performance culture than a written culture, "kissing" had more legal than lustful connotations.[8] To swear on the Bible one "kissed the book." "A kissing" was how the early Middle Ages designated the procedure whereby a bond was created between lord and vassal or knight. By kissing the vassal or knight full on the mouth, the lord was making him "a man of mouth and hands." Transfers of property were made legal, and disputes were settled, by the seal of the kiss. The same goes for people taking office. The original function of the ritual kiss between bride and groom was the creation of a legal relationship, not romance.[9]

HOLY KISS

In Christianity the kiss had an almost sacramental function from the start. "Greet one another with a kiss," Paul says, making it almost into a liturgical observance (2 Cor. 13:12). Almost all the earliest liturgies of the church mention the kiss. The kiss was a sacred and sacramental sign of love. Not of peace, but of love.

There was a lot of kissing going on in the early church. Clement of Alexandria complained that there was too much kissing. He said there were those "who do nothing but make the churches resound with a kiss."[10]

A close reading of the New Testament makes it seem almost like that: father kissing son when he returned from his waywardness (Luke 15:20); church members greeting one another with a kiss (Rom. 16:16; 1 Cor. 16:20; 2 Cor. 13:12; 1 Thess. 5:26); Mary Magdalen kissing the feet of Jesus; Jesus reproaching Simon the Pharisee for not greeting him with a kiss after inviting and receiving him into his house (Luke 7:45)—Jesus dared to receive kisses of love even from disreputable characters. When Paul left the elders of Ephesus, they showered him with kisses.

The noun *kiss* is mentioned seven times in the New Testament, twice in Luke. The verb *kiss* appears six times: once each in Matthew (26:49) and Mark (14:45) in connection with Judas and three times in Luke. The command to kiss appears four times in Paul and once in 1 Peter.

Two Great Kisses

There are two great kisses in Christian theology.

The first great kiss is when God breathed into humans the breath of life. When the ancient writers wanted to convey union not physically but spiritually, they used the metaphor of the kiss. William of Saint Thierry developed this notion of the kiss as a sign of unity: the Holy Spirit was the kiss of the Father and the Son; Jesus was the kiss of the Creator and creation.

In the kiss of God and humans, the two parties exchanged breath. God breathed the spirit (*pneuma*) into Adam. God kissed Adam, and in so doing blew the very breath of life into him (Gen. 2:7). The creation scene in early Christian art often includes a ray of light that runs from God's mouth to Adam's mouth. In the rabbinic tradition, it was argued that there were righteous persons (Moses, Enoch, Elisha) who were translated into heaven directly by the kiss of God. Eternity is the perfect kiss that flows from the union of the soul and God.

The second great kiss is when Jesus breathed into the disciples new life in the Holy Spirit. Augustine said the mystic kiss symbolism became explicit in John 20:21–22 NIV. When Jesus "breathed" upon the disciples and said "Receive the Holy Spirit," Augustine interpreted this to mean that Jesus exhaled life into the disciples and passed on the Spirit to them through the gesture of a kiss.

What was behind one of the most ancient and unique rituals of the early church? What was behind the notion of those first Christians? It was unthinkable that you would greet one another without touching one another.

† † †

> A kiss conveys the force of love, and where there is no love, no faith, no affection, what sweetness can there be in kisses?
>
> —Saint Ambrose[11]

† † †

Judas Kiss

We are given a clue in Jesus' hurt questioning of Judas: "Judas, would you betray the Son of Man with a kiss?" (Luke 22:48 NEB). The issue for Jesus was not so much Judas's betrayal. Peter betrayed Jesus. Thomas betrayed Jesus. In one fashion or another all the disciples betrayed him. The trouble Jesus had with Judas was betrayal—"with a kiss?"

Betrayal with a kiss makes Judas's betrayal one of the most powerful ever to have gripped the human imagination.[12] To this day the kiss of peace is omitted from the mass on Holy Thursday as an expression of horror at the Judas kiss of betrayal.

Scholars have discussed for centuries why Judas betrayed Jesus with a kiss. Why this treachery? Jesus didn't need to be identified. Everybody knew who Jesus was. Maybe Judas led them to Jesus' hiding place? But what kind of a "hiding place" was the Garden? And even then, why didn't Judas just give the signal by pointing out or pointing to Jesus?

Holy Kiss

There is one explanation that puts everything into focus. The kiss was an insider sign and seal. It is not accurate for us to designate this the "kiss of peace," as the *New English Bible* renders it. It is more precisely the "holy kiss." And this "holy kiss" was a distinctive mark of the early Christians. The practice must have originated from their experience with Jesus himself.

The kiss symbolized to the ancient Christians the transmission of the Spirit—its passing on and surpassing power. Following the consecration of the Eucharist, the priest spoke the words *pax vobiscum*, after which the members of the body of Christ would kiss one another. Thus they became one in the spirit, enabling them to receive the eucharistic body of Christ as "one body and one soul" and be incorporated into his spirit.

It is difficult for us to understand just how unique this ritual was. Talmudic rabbis knew three kinds of kisses: greeting, leave-taking, and respect. But such kisses were carefully ritualized and circumscribed. According to New Testament scholar William Klassen, Paul himself was "the first popular ethical teacher known to instruct members of a mixed social group to continue to greet each other with a kiss whenever or wherever they meet."[13] What is more, "there is no basis in ancient texts, Jewish and Greco-Roman, outside the New Testament for the transformation of the kiss into a sign of religious community. There is no analogy in any body of religious literature to this practice commended by two writers of the New Testament."[14]

Klassen is convinced that the ritual of the "holy kiss"

> began as a practice which expressed the closeness of people who were coming from many different social classes and who were transcending gender, religious, national, and ethnic divisions and finding themselves one in Christ. Such an emerging social reality called for new practices and new ways of communication . . . new forms of greeting, in the market place, on the streets, at the forum and in their homes when they gathered for worship. Just as Jesus had provided new forms of greeting and new guidance on greeting (Matt.10:12; Luke 10:5–6) so here the early Christians were urged to greet each other within the context of their relationship to a Holy God. They saw themselves as "in Christ." That new level of reality was being affirmed in the freedom of quite innocently greeting each other with a holy kiss. They risked the slander of those who were outside looking in—every new social group takes that risk if it is to survive. But there was also a considerable amount of social bonding power in establishing this new way of expressing love for each other.[15]

The ritual of the "holy kiss" was a way of symbolizing to rich and poor, men and women, clean and unclean, old and young, morally pure and morally not so pure, that they were loved by God beyond anything they could imagine and that God's Spirit played no favorites. In short, Klassen concludes, "The 'holy kiss' is a public declaration of the affirmation of faith: 'In Christ there is neither male nor female, Jew nor Greek, slave nor free' (Gal. 3:28)."[16]

In Dostoevsky's *The Brothers Karamazov* there is a tale in which Jesus comes back to earth during the Inquisition and the Grand Inquisitor puts him on trial for all of his failures. After the Inquisitor makes a full and complete case against Jesus, filled with canny arguments and shrewd charges, it is Jesus' turn.

Jesus' only response is to go over to the grim and menacing attacker and kiss him. No dazzling reasoning, no wonder-working displays. The essence of Christianity lies in this simple but profound act: love in the face of hate.[17]

Hands Off

The right foot of a statue of Peter in Saint Peter's Square is almost gone because so many people have kissed it. The essence of the kiss is the sense of touch. Of the five senses, smell, then taste, and the highest of all—touch—were the most exalted senses from a spiritual perspective. Sight and sound have been deemed the lowest of the spiritual senses. Saint Thomas Aquinas made touch the most elemental sense.[18]

Jesus had a touching ministry. Jesus' ministry was very physical. For Jesus touching was a primary carrier of spiritual truth.

If you don't touch a baby, what happens? It dies. Literally. If a child hasn't learned to hug and kiss by the age of two, there are serious indications that one of two things is wrong: neurological damage, or autism.[19] *Marasmus* is the technical word for wasting away in infants when not given sufficient touch. One of the most powerful pieces of literature ever written on marasmus is this poem by Frederick Leboyer:

> Touching, yes, is the root . . .
> We have to feed babies,
> Fill them both
> inside and outside.
> We must speak to their skins . . .
> which thirst and hunger
> and cry
> as much as their bellies.
> We must gorge them
> with warmth and caresses
> just as we do with milk.[20]

One physician has even argued that he would rather choose as a life partner "any number of brain-damaged people, rather than one unbonded person, for we are *flexible* beyond measure and can compensate for extensive physical damage, but lack of bonding finds no compensation."[21] One of the most frightening statistics for the future is the decline of touching in family settings. In USAmerica, parents touch their kids only about two times per hour on average. In France, parents touch their kids six times per hour.[22]

Researchers have been focused on studying the ways in which tactile stimulation is a powerful stimulant to infant growth and child development.23 But touch is essential to the elderly as well, especially those with impairments. Some scientists have argued that the need for touch may even supercede an elderly person's need to talk.

In the light of recent research that points to the importance of touch, how ironic that throughout the modern era, and especially during the high modern era of the twentieth century, we have been in retreat from touching. In the words of legal scholar Bernard J. Hibbitts, "We have largely struck touch from our cultural canon. . . . Sight has displaced touch as a preferred arbiter of knowledge."24 The old adage, "Seeing is believing," actually began as an endorsement of touch as a carrier of truth: "Seeing is believing, but feeling's the truth."

High-modern culture is a touch-free culture with touch-free everything, even touch-free bathrooms. There are workshops to help make the church more "touch-free" and "hands off." The line is a straight one: the more touch-starved the culture, the more touch crimes we can expect. The statistics are bearing this out. In the words of one abused German patient, "The absence of loving touch and the abundance of sadistic sexual touch has badly wounded me. Man does not live by breath alone."25

In spite of all the "Hands Off!" cultural discourse, it could be argued that *not touching* is a form of abuse, a form of neglect.26

Doubt the power of touch? What do you do when you are angry with someone? You "avoid contact" with them. What do you do with "touchy" people? You "avoid contact" with them.

We are a touching people. Disciples of Jesus cannot be out of touch with touching. The church cannot lose touch with touching. You can't heal people without touching them. A Jesus you can't touch is a Jesus who can't save. For Jesus to be our Savior, he first must be our toucher.

A physician, Joanna Seibert, wrote a letter to a church magazine. I clipped it out and taped it in my notebook. This is her story:

> Today I visited an eight-year-old girl dying of cancer. Her body was disfigured by her disease and its treatment. She was in almost constant pain. As I entered her room, I was overcome almost immediately by her suffering—so unjust, unfair, unreasonable. Even more overpowering [however] was the presence of her grandmother lying in bed beside her with her huge body embracing this precious, inhuman suffering.
>
> I stood in awe, for I knew I was on holy ground. . . . The suffering of innocent children is horrifying beyond words. I will never forget the great, gentle arms and body of this grandmother. She never spoke while I was there. She was holding and participating in suffering that she could not relieve, and somehow her silent presence was relieving it. No words could express the magnitude of her love.

The church of Jesus Christ "stays in touch." Christianity is a contact culture, a tactile religion.[27] Biblical spirituality is a contact sport. Each human hand has 1.5 million receptors: God made the hand for healing and touching. The key is not so much knowing when to touch as knowing when *not* to touch and knowing how never to remove the tact from the tactile.

Touch Me Not, but Touch Me

The passage from John 20:17 where Jesus says, "Touch me not yet . . ." is called "one of the most perplexing sections in the Gospel"[28] and one of "a handful of the most difficult passages in the New Testament."[29] It is a strange warning Jesus gives to Mary Magdalen: "Cease to touch me, for I am not yet ascended to the Father."

In this charge to "touch me not yet" the words *not yet* are as much a key as Jesus' command *me mou haptou* ("touch me not," which is better than "don't cling to me"). "Touch me *not yet*" implies that after the Ascension one actually can touch Jesus. After Christ has ascended, it will be possible for Mary, for the disciples, for others to touch him. By ascending, Jesus opens up for us the possibility of a new relationship with him through the Spirit.[30]

How? How can touching be possible after the Ascension? How can we touch Jesus when he is not there? And why does he tell Mary Magdalene not to touch him in the morning, when in the evening he invites Thomas to touch his wounded side?[31]

Is it possible that Jesus is promising to give his disciples a new relationship with God whereby we can in some way touch God?

How? First, through the Eucharist, where we touch his body and blood.[32] And second, through "Inasmuch," where "inasmuch as you have done it unto the least of these, you have done it unto me." Jesus promised that perfect freedom comes not to those who do as they please but to those who love as they should. Touch here, and you touch there, and you touch everywhere, even the heavens themselves. By touching those in need, we touch Jesus himself through the power of the Holy Spirit.

† † †

Cookin' hard, kissin' hard.
>   —Old Amish expression

† † †

God's Kiss

The father kissed the prodigal son, as God (the Father) embraces and kisses us who are prodigals. How? Through Jesus, God's Kiss to Earth. As a parent kisses a child's hurt to "make it better," so God kisses our hurts to make us better through Jesus the Christ, God's kiss of love. We in turn are called to be the "kiss of the kiss" (St. Bernard of Clairvaux), reproducing in our lives God's "heartquake" for the world and God's "heartquake" for us.[33]

† † †

*The combined energy of God's spirit and their love
for one another and for those outsiders was irresistible.*
>   —Charles Cousar

† † †

The artist, Benjamin West, traces the beginnings of his career as a painter to a boyhood incident with his little niece Sally. His mother and sister left him in charge of the sleeping Sally while they went out to pick flowers in the garden.

While he was fanning her to keep the flies away, he noticed her beautiful smile as she slept. He discovered several bottles of colored ink and some paper and proceeded to draw her portrait. When he heard his mother and sister returning, he tried his best to hide what he was doing, but his suspicious mother demanded to see what he had been doing.

Instead of being angry, when she saw the drawing, she examined it carefully and exclaimed, "I declare he has made a likeness of little Sally." And then she kissed Ben.[34]

"And ever since that day," Benjamin West is reported to have said, "my mother's encouraging kiss in the dark made me a painter."

Jesus is God's "kiss in the dark." Our lives, like Jesus himself, like Paul's epistles, are a kind of "kiss of love" from heaven to earth and "kiss in the dark" to those who are hiding and afraid and in trouble. Jesus brought together people hiding in the dark—people who never talked together, people who never ate together, people who never drank together, even people who never touched each other—and Jesus brought them into the light, showed them one another, and showed them a way of greater sanity, a way of greater sanctity.

Jesus turned "others" into "anothers." Jesus never knew an "untouchable." There are no untouchables, church. No one is so down and out . . . No one is so up and out . . . to be out of touch with the touch of Christ. Untouchability is not in any Christian's dictionary.

"Preloved" is.

"Preloved"

There is a new word in the *1999 Encarta World English Dictionary*, a venture between Bill Gates's Microsoft and Bloomsbury Publishing of London. There are a lot of varieties of English spoken by those 750 million around the world (British, USAmerican, Canadian, Caribbean, Scottish, Irish, Welsh, South African, South Asian, Southeast Asian, Australian, and New Zealand) who now speak English, and the one billion who are currently learning the *lingua franca* of the New World. The new word comes from Australia and New Zealand. That word is *preloved*. *Preloved* specifically means an article for sale secondhand. But more figuratively, *preloved* means embracing something ahead of time so that it arrives well wrapped in appreciation and well cared for.

Let's put Jesus' principles of "no untouchables" and "preloved" to the test. Do this little exercise. Close your eyes and bring to mind the face of the most pitiful excuse for a human being you can come up with. The test is this: Can you kiss that person with God's love?

Can the church kiss Dennis Rodman? Can we say, "I love Dennis Rodman. I love Rodzilla."

Can the church kiss Marilyn Manson? Can we say, "I love Marilyn Manson?"

Can the church kiss Howard Stern? Can we say, "I love Howard Stern?"

Can the church reach out and touch the untouchables?

The first rock opera *Tommy* (1969) was written by Pete Townshend and the WHO. The story revolves around a deaf, dumb, and blind pinball-playing boy whose limitations were parallel to our own inability to use our higher senses. In the song "Christmas," the father talks about his son who doesn't know what Christmas morning means, who

> doesn't know what day it is.
> He doesn't know who Jesus was
> Or what praying is.
> How can he be saved
> From the eternal grave?
> Tommy, can you hear me?
> Tommy, can you hear me?
> Tommy, can you hear me?
> How can he be saved?

Suddenly Tommy responds to his father:

> See me, feel me, touch me, heal me!
> See me, feel me, touch me, heal me!

There is a culture out there saying in a million ways, "See me, feel me, touch me, heal me!"

Can we touch this culture? Can we kiss it?

The "official" release of the last words from the Space Shuttle *Challenger* to Houston Control had someone exclaiming "uh-oh." An "unofficial" transcript of the final communication with the *Challenger* crew reveals that all aboard knew what was happening, and the panic in their voices was palpable. In this "unofficial" communication with the spacecraft, the last words spoken on the *Challenger* are from one of the astronauts: "Give me your hand."

I believe in the touch of the human hand.

I believe even more in the healing touch of Jesus the Christ.

When parents put their children to bed, they kiss their kids goodnight.

Parents kiss their kids goodnight.

Christians kiss their world awake.

Jesus' last words were these: "You will bear witness for me" (Acts 1:8 REB).

In other words, kiss and tell.

Kiss and tell. Don't go kiss and tell it on the mountain.

Go kiss and tell it on Main Street.

Go kiss and tell it on Wall Street.

Go kiss and tell it on Bourbon Street.

Go kiss and tell it on the streets of Calcutta.

Faith Practices and Web Interactives

1. Listen to Faith Hill's album *Faith* and her hit single on it, "Kiss."

2. Have someone read and review Christopher Nyrop's book *The Kiss and Its History* (London: Sands, 1901; repr. Detroit: Singing Tree Press, 1968).

3. The Bible says that the crowds tried to touch Jesus, "for power came out from him and healed them." There is power in the healing touch of Jesus—power to hold us, power to carry us, power to lead us, power to heal us.

What is keeping you from touching this culture with the gospel of Jesus Christ?

4. As part of a contest in the winter of 1997, a Maryland man spent fifty-nine hours kissing a motorboat. The prize? He got to keep the boat.

What are you kissing?

5. Listen to the song sung by Ingrid Bergman and Humphrey Bogart in *Casablanca* (1942): "A kiss is still a kiss . . . No matter what the future brings . . . As time goes by."

No matter what the future brings, what is your church doing to ensure that the world can count on your kiss?

6. Evaluate the following statement: "Given today's world, it is nearly impossible to raise a secure, happy, healthy child who is untainted by the ills of contemporary culture. Even if well-intentioned parents manage to create a loving home; even if their children's bodies do not become overly toxified by the chemicals in the food and water that they ingest, or the radiation emissions from their television sets, these children are still going to be faced with the toxic and often cruel world that is just outside their doorstep."[35]

7. In some preliterate cultures, people made an X mark instead of their signature. But in medieval times what made that X mark binding, the way legal documents bind us today, was the act of kissing the X. In other words, kissing the X was what scholars today call "performance law," a ritual act witnessed by the person who wrote the text. It functioned as an oath to guarantee that whatever obligations were stated in the document would be carried out.

8. Are you prepared for the new, upcoming meaning to "reach out and touch someone." Very shortly you will be able to exchange information with a handshake. In fact, the Media Lab at MIT has already done this by putting transmitters in shoes and letting the body act as a "wet wire" which enables data to be transferred directly to each other's receivers.[36]

9. The Conservative Mennonites still practice the holy kiss after foot-washing. What other evidences of the "holy kiss" are still evident in Christianity?

10. Compare the Gaither Vocal Band's (with Janet Paschal) rendition of "Tell Me" with SixPence None the Richer's hit single "Kiss Me" (Squint Entertainment, 1998— featured in the Miramax motion picture *She's All That*).

Why do you think this particular Christian song made it to the top of the secular charts? Discuss the thesis that both songs are exactly the same except "Tell Me" is for a churched audience, and "Kiss Me" is pitched to a pre-Christian crowd.

11. Constantin Brancusi's *The Kiss* (c. 1910), one of the two most famous kiss sculptures in the history of art, was actually carved from a single stone. You can see it at the Philadelphia Museum of Art. Can you identify the other kiss sculpture?

12. In 1989, Moorhead State University in Minnesota banned mistletoe on the grounds that it encouraged sexual harassment.

13. "If I have laid my hand on my mouth to kiss [i.e. to show respect to a heathen god], 'let this also be reckoned to me as the greatest crime'" (Job 31:27–28, paraphrased).

14. Check out these twelve exemplary postmodern Web sites:

www.drinkdeep.org
www.ginghamsburg.org
www.theooze.com
www.tcpc.org
www.phutrue.com
www.sofn.org.uk
www.alphalink.com.au/~pashton/essays/postmodernism.htm
www.cs.cmu.edu/afs/cs.cmu.edu/user/phoebe/mosaic/postmodernism
www.crossrds.org/gloss.htm
www.crossrds.org/dotrel.htm
www.jordoncooper.homepage.com/postmodern.html

For an excellent example of a church Web site that has morphed into a Webzine and online resource, see Bellview Baptist's ("the cure for the common church") *www.bellview.org/index.asp*

15. Peter Sheldrup has an excellent video for group discussion called *Postmodern Pilgrims*. Call 360-756-1094 to order a copy or send a $20 check to Peter Sheldrupt, 2804 Williams Street, Bellingham, WA 98225.

16. The number of songs with hand-holding themes is legion. For example, Here is

> "Hold my hand, just hold my hand . . .
> Because I want to love you, the best that,
> the best that I can."
> —Hootie and the Blowfish, "Hold My Hand"

What other songs with hand-holding lyrics can you think of? Play them and discuss their "theologies."

† † †

Chapter One

EPIC Church for Epic Times

E(xperiential)-P-I-C

eBay

I am an eBay addict.

My most recent purchase is one of the first books published by my Ph.D. adviser. It has been missing from my library for twenty years. I got it for $.50. The postage was more than the book ($2.00). But for $2.50 I felt like I had just reclaimed a lost part of my pedigree. I felt like a kid in a candy store.

Amazon.com and eBay.com are the wonder stories of the '90s. From 1995 to 1999, online auction giant eBay did no advertising, no marketing, yet boasted 6 million registered users and grew from 289,000 items at the end of 1996 to 3.6 million today. With a 23 billion market cap, eBay is now worth more than K-mart, Toys "R" Us, Nordstrom, and Saks combined.

eBay is so addictive because it understands postmodern culture better than the church. eBay also alerts us to what the church must do to get the attention and attendance of postmoderns. For the church to incarnate the gospel in this postmodern world, it must become more medieval than modern, more apostolic than patristic. I call postmodernity an EPIC culture: Experiential, Participatory, Image-driven, Connected.

In the midst of one of the greatest transitions in history—from modern to postmodern—Christian churches are owned lock, stock, and barrel by modernity.[1] They have clung to modern modes of thought and action, their ways of embodying and enacting the Christian tradition frozen in patterns of high modernity.

The decline of western Christianity is so well documented it needs no rehearsing here.[2] The annual meetings of most churches are like that of the swimming coach who made a difficult speech at an awards banquet after a disastrous year. "We didn't win a single meet this year," he admitted, "but we had a good time and nobody drowned." The plight of mainline Protestantism has passed into the realm of humor. At a recent board meeting of a community agency, someone used the phrase "mainline churches." Someone else asked, "What are mainline churches?" A third snapped back, "The ones with the fewest people."

For the first time in USAmerican history more people are attending nondenominational than denominationally affiliated churches.[3] In one year alone (1997–98), average church size plummeted over 10 percent, with a drop of 15 percent during the same twelve-month period in annual operating budgets.[4] Eighty-five percent of the mainline church is in serious deterioration or comatose. Wonder who are the biggest losers in terms of percent change in weekday activities from 1981 to 1997? For girls ages three through twelve, the four biggest losers were outdoor activities (-57%), conversations (-55%), free play (-26%), and church (-25%). For boys ages three through twelve, the four biggest losers were church (-71%), outdoor activities (-70%), conversations (-60%), and free play (-34%).[5]

I have a friend—one of the most successful pastors in the South—who has a metaphor for the church's plight. He says the church's leaders have Alzheimer's disease. We still love them. We remember and pass on their stories. But they're living in another world. They're totally clueless about the world that is actually out there. The problem is, he laments, they're captaining the ship.

My favorite example of how out of touch the church can be with the emerging postmodern world around it is a throwaway line from Marc Driscoll, Gen-X pastor at Seattle's thriving Mars Hill Fellowship (which is itself planting three more churches). Driscoll says his challenge in reaching postmoderns is not convincing them that Jesus rose from the dead or that there could be such a thing as a resurrection. His biggest challenge is in convincing postmoderns that there was only *one* resurrection.

Western Christianity went to sleep in a modern world governed by the gods of reason and observation. It is awakening to a postmodern world open to revelation and hungry for experience. Indeed, one of the last places postmoderns expect to be "spiritual" is the church. In the midst of a spiritual "heating up" in the host postmodern culture, the church is stuck in the modern freezer.

The church's crisis is of EPIC proportions. It will take more than a Martha Stewart makeover or spiritual plastic surgery to make church vital to a postmodern culture. Unless churches can transition their cultures into more EPIC directions—Experiential, Participatory, Image-based, and Connected—they stand the real risk of becoming museum churches, nostalgic testimonies to a culture that is no more.

This book begins with chapters of cultural analysis devoted to what each one of these words means in that acronym EPIC. The book ends with a more theoretical analysis of the social forces and intellectual figures fashioning this EPIC model.

✝ ✝ ✝

Some people want to see God with their eyes as they see a cow, and to love him as they love their cow—they love their cow for the milk and cheese and profit it makes them. This is how it is with people who love God for the sake of outward wealth or inward comfort. They do not rightly love God when they love him for their own advantage. Indeed, I tell you the truth, any object you have on your mind, however good, will be a barrier between you and the inmost Truth.
—Dominican mystic Meister Eckhart[6]

✝ ✝ ✝

Experiential: From Rational to Experiential

Toward the end of his life, the great Dominican theologian Thomas Aquinas had a direct experience of God's love. From that moment on, Aquinas stopped writing and called everything he had written "all grass."

It is one thing to talk about God. It is quite another thing to experience God.

A modernist dies and finds himself surrounded by dense, billowy clouds that only allow him to see a short distance ahead. He sees that he is walking down a road paved in gold. Ahead, there is a slight break in the clouds. He sees a signpost and a fork in the road. The signpost has inscriptions with golden arrows pointing to the left and right.

The modernist reads them. The right arrow says, "This way to heaven." The left arrow says, "This way to a discussion about heaven."

The modernist took the fork to the discussion.

Guess which fork the postmodernist took?

The perpetual openness to experience of postmoderns is such that one can never underestimate the e-factor: experiential. Postmoderns will do most anything not to lose connection with the experience of life.

The magic of eBay is that it makes shopping an experience. There's a homegrown feel to eBay. Journalist Stewart Alsop, while analyzing the eBay phenomenon, calls it "nail-biting, thrilling fun."[7]

✝ ✝ ✝

There is no doubt that all our knowledge begins with experience.
   —Beginning of Kant's *Critique of Pure Reason*[8]

✝ ✝ ✝

Experience Currencies

The postmodern economy is an "experience economy."[9] Some call this "immersion living." Others call it "The Emotile Era." But whatever you call it, experience is the currency of postmodern economics. In the last half century much of the world has transitioned from an industrial economy (driven by things) to a knowledge economy (driven by bits) to an experience economy (which traffics in experiences).

✝ ✝ ✝

Sometimes you cannot believe what you see, you have to believe what you feel.
  —*Brandeis professor Morrie Schwartz to Mitch Albom in* Tuesdays with Morrie[10]

✝ ✝ ✝

The precise nature of this new experience economy has been summarized exquisitely by Marilyn Carlson Nelson, the chair, president, and CEO of Carlson Companies, one of the world's largest privately held companies:

Anyone who views a sale as a transaction is going to be toast down the line. Selling is not about peddling a product. It's about wrapping that product in a service—and about selling both the product and the service as an experience. That approach to selling helps create a vital element of the process: a relationship. In a world where things move at hyperspeed, what was relevant yesterday may not be relevant tomorrow. But one thing that endures is a dynamic relationship that is grounded in an experience that you've provided.[11]

What keeps shoppers returning to a store? The products? Or the experience? As one patron said as he walked away from a new Greenwich Village eatery called Peanut Butter & Co., "This is very much an experience; it's not just a sandwich."[12]

Moderns want to figure out what life's about. Postmoderns want to experience what life is, especially experience life for themselves. Postmoderns are not willing to live at even an arms'-length distance from experience. They want life to explode all around them. Postmoderns don't want their information straight. They want it laced with experience (hence edutainment). And the more extreme the better.

Tom Beaudoin, a body-pierced Gen-X Christian with a theology degree from Harvard, says that piercing/tattooing "reflects the centrality of personal and intimate experience in Xers' lives." Tattooing is a "marking" of a spiritual experience, a "branding" in a body-oriented "brand" culture.[13]

Already USAmerican consumers spend more on entertainment than on health care or clothing.[14] In fact, USAmericans have dedicated more and more of their budgets for entertainment ever since 1987.[15] Can you guess what age group is spending the most? Whenever critics tell me that the "postmodern thing" is but a generational phenomenon, I like to point out that those under age thirty-five account for a lesser share of spending on entertainment than USAmericans aged fifty-five and older. According to sociologists:

> It's the senior citizens who have become America's true party animals. The average household headed by a 65-to-74 year old spends more on entertainment than does the average household headed by someone under age 25. Even the very oldest householders are in on this revolution: Those aged 75-plus spent 98 percent more on entertainment in 1997 than in 1987, the biggest increase of any age group.[16]

Whatever happened to the fountain pen? They're leaking ink all over computers. Ask Mont Blanc how much high-tech postmoderns want high-touch experiences with their fingers. Theme restaurants are popping up everywhere. Recently opened are Crash Café in Baltimore, where you will eat to the sounds of crash sites, and Igor's in Hong Kong, a haunted castle where human skeletons will serve you. To keep its "experiences" fresh, The Gap introduces a new product line every six to eight weeks. An "experienced car" is now the preferred term for what used to be called "used car" or "pre-owned car." One car company offers customers the experience of having their next car test-drive by race-car drivers.

† † †

They're all taking it rather well, kind of excited.
Vacationers, new experiences—what can I say?
—Jacob Naylor, night manager of Joshua Tree Hotel
when asked how guests coped with the crisisof a 7.0
earthquake in October 1999 that rocked southern
California and knocked out their power[17]

† † †

REI's "flagship" store in Seattle looks more like a retail amusement park than a store. One of the country's largest wilderness-sports stores (100,000 square feet, 60,000 stock items), the consumer cooperative Recreational Equipment Inc. (REI) boasts places for customers to interact with and experience some of the products they are selling—a seven-story climbing wall; a 300-foot waterfall; a 475-foot-long biking trail and test track; a 100-seat café; a rain room for testing how waterproof the Leak-Tex is; a lab where camp stoves can be tried out; etc. The aisles between departments are designed to resemble hiking trails.

Honda has based an entire sales strategy on an "experiential" foundation. Honda's success with its four hundred supplier companies throughout North America is based on what they call "The Three Joys." According to "The Three Joys," each component in the "car experience" (customer, employee, supplier) should enjoy the "experience." Customers should have a positive experience of ownership. The dealer who connects the customer to the supplier should enjoy the experience of bringing pleasure to the customer—high customer satisfaction. Honda, who supplies the product, should enjoy the experience of pleasing both other parties with such a superb product.

† † †

Engineering. Science. Technology. All worthless . . . unless they make you feel something.
—ad for BMW's 3 Series cars

† † †

Experience Industries

John A. Quelch, dean of the London Business School, the leading business school outside North America, says that "we're not in the education business. We're in the transformation business. We expect everyone who participates in a program at the London Business School . . . to be transformed by the experience."[18] The outcome measurement for this prestigious educational institution is a simple one: have we created "a transformative experience?"

Why is tourism one of if not *the* fastest-growing industry in the world? It creates a new job every 2.5 seconds and generates investments of $3.2 billion *a day*. Annually, $1.9 trillion is spent on tourism worldwide, accounting for one-tenth of the global economic impact and more than 350 million employees by 2005.[19]

Some scholars interpret the touristic phenomenon as a postmodern ritual that performs the same role as sacred rites did in premodern societies. Heritage tourism appeals to a culture's search for "authenticity," "otherness," "identity," and educational experiences while vacationing.

In 1994, 528 million people traveled for the pleasure of experiences of "otherness." By 2010, this figure is expected to rise to 937 million. Half the world's vacationers head to the sea each year—and half the world's people live within fifty miles or so of salt water. But tourism has reached every region of the globe—from the mountains to the desert, from the polar ice caps to the tropical rain forests. It will soon reach the moon first and then Mars. What will get us there will not be government space agencies but Hilton and Ritz-Carlton.[20]

Why is travel and tourism the U.S.'s largest export industry as well as our second largest employer (after health) and third largest retail industry (after automotive and food store sales)?

Why? Because tourism is an experience industry. The fastest growing segment of tourism is adventure travel, with more than two hundred travel books appearing each month catering to this clientele. Adventure travel will likely become in our lifetimes the largest commercial use of space once reusable launchers reduce costs sufficiently for space tours to orbiting space stations.[21] It is not surprising that in an experience economy frequent mall shopping would plummet, down from 16 percent in 1987 to less than 10 percent in 1998. Yet at the same time the Mall of America (Bloomington, Minnesota) "now hosts more visitors than Walt Disney World, Disneyland, and the Grand Canyon *combined*."[22] Why? It's not a mall, but an experience center. The same is true for Nashville's OpryMills, which opened in May 2000. A day at the spa is not enough. There must be body salts from Israel, or muds from Turkey and the Oran Sea.

Soul Quests

This is not the first time there has been this pursuit of dreams, emotions, and extreme experience. Look at the crusades; every expression of romanticism in history has been a tilting towards the experiential. But never before has the trafficking in experience become the primary currency of a global economic system and the downloading of trivial experience, the new holy grail.

American Demographics esteemed the quest for "experiential faith" and the rediscovery of the soul so pervasive ("one of the nation's most important cultural trends") that it did a cover issue on the phenomenon.[23] We are spending two billion dollars a year on self-help resources alone: books, videos, tapes, and seminars.[24] When the "spirituality" and "self-help" categories are combined, the numbers are truly staggering.

✝ ✝ ✝

Luxury isn't the key to happiness. . . . True luxury . . . is living a spiritual life.
                                        —Massage therapist Patrick Bishop[25]

✝ ✝ ✝

Spirituality is now rubbing shoulders with quacks and respectable scholars in unpredictable ways. Serious biographers in academic treatises are proposing that Gore Vidal is a reincarnation of their subject (in this case William Beckford).[26] There is an explosion of inspirational art, from New Age to Native American. In fact, someone estimated that if one divides the number of art pieces sold by the "light painter" Thomas Kincade into the number of USAmericans, one in five of us own one of his paintings.

The Clemmer Group, a North American network of personal-improvement experts, has concluded that the twenty-first century is the dawning of a massive "spiritual awakening." According to a ten-year study reported by Dow Jones & Company, there is a new paradigm for living among about forty-four million USAmericans who are heavily invested and involved in campaigns of spiritual awareness.

Yet fewer and fewer are turning to the church for guidance in this soul quest.[27] A spiritual awakening is taking place in the culture largely outside the Christian church partly because churches, in the words of award-winning journalist Chip Brown, "were more interested in repressing ecstatic experience than in nurturing it. Rapture, not to say healing, was certainly not on the agenda of the church I was packed off to each Sunday morning."[28]

The number of unchurched adults is rising. The Barna Research Group defines an "unchurched" adult as someone who has not attended a Christian church service during the past six months other than for a wedding, funeral, or holiday service. What it finds is that the numbers of unchurched USAmericans rose from 27 percent in January 1998 to 31 percent in June 1999. That's a 4 percent rise in eighteen months, or eight million new unchurched adults nationwide in a year and a half.[29] The areas of greatest increase in the unchurched? The South (up from 19 percent to 26 percent), the Gen-Xers (up from 31 to 39 percent), and men (up from 33 to 40 percent).[30] When asked their religious preference, 19 percent of Xers said "none," compared with 12 percent of baby boomers and 7 percent of the Silent (Swing) Generation and 4 percent of the GI (WWII) Generation.[31]

Cultural Thievery

Ironically, the spiritual awakening in the culture is being fueled by siphoning off stuff from our own tanks and then remixing it for popular culture.

Is the world stealing our best lines? Or have we given them away[32]—unable to see their relevance to the world in which we live. So we leave them lying there for others to pick up.

And pick them up they do. I first noticed the church's flubbing of its own lines and failure to speak plain and simple with the hit television series *Cheers*. Is there anyone who doesn't know the tag line for the *Cheers* bar: "Where everybody knows your name." Does that have a faintly familiar ring?

The movie *Field of Dreams* was my next wake-up call to cultural thievery from the church's treasure chest. Again, does anybody *not* know the theme image for the movie? "Build it, and they will come." The faintly familiar feel to this line was brought home after a cursory concordance search unearthed Haggai 1:8: "Build my house, and I will come in all my glory" (my paraphrase). Not build some fantasy field and fantasy figures will show up. But build God's house, and the maker of heaven and earth will appear in all the Creator's splendor and power.

The "No Fear" logo is shameless embezzlement. In one form or another 365 times the Scriptures admonish us to "fear not," "be not afraid"—and not just when angels appear. Are we so tone deaf to the sounds of postmodern culture that we can't translate "fear not" into "no fear"?

Nike's "Do It" slogan is a direct lift from Christian texts and traditions. Instead of a narcissistic slogan that encourages you to do whatever you want to do, the biblical injunctions to "do it" tell us what to do and what not to do, why we should "do it," for whom we should "do it," what happens when we don't "do it." When the culture plunders our images, it twists and distorts them so that they mean something else.

This is only the tip of the iceberg. Volvo wants to "save your soul." Lotus and Caldwell Banker introduced in 1999 the same marketing slogan: "I am, I am." Allianz lyricizes, to hymnic music, "Wherever you go, I will be with you." The words *spirit* and *spiritual* are now marketing terms, as

Madison Avenue plays on this pervasive sense that reason cannot address the deeper things of life.

What *isn't* "spirit" something or other? There are now even "spiritual" cosmetics. You can bathe in "I Trust" bubble bath, and moisturize your body with "Bliss" (Chakra VII by Aveda), for "the joyful enlightenment and soaring of the spirit." Then you can put on the powder "Rebirth" by 5S "to renew the spirit and recharge the soul." Don't forget the nail polish "Spiritual" (by Tony and Tina) to "aid connection with the higher self." One '90s TV commercial showed a bearded welder naming his relationship with his Mazda truck "a spiritual thing."

Corporate culture is seizing biblical images and doctrines and inventing a "New Reformation" and "New Economy" based on them. B. Joseph White, dean of the University of Michigan Business School, says that "business is the most powerful, most progressive social force in the world."[33] I blanche when I hear this and blush that the same thing isn't being said about the church. But it is the corporate sector that is now promoting "servant leadership." Every company has a "mission" and "mission statement." Businesses like Ecotrust have job positions called "circuit riders."[34] Developers are building communities that are "covenant protected." And the ultimate in effective marketing is called "viral marketing," which relies on word of mouth and pass-it-on for spreading. Isn't that how the gospel first spread, as well as the most biblical form of evangelism: viral evangelism?

Most amazing of all, one of the most problematic words for some segments of the church, evangelism, is now the hottest business buzzword. Corporations are hiring "evangelists," and CEOs are restyling their job descriptions to be seen as "evangelists." Guy Kawasaki, former "marketing evangelist" for Apple Computer, wrote *Rules for Revolutionaries* (1998)[35] in which he helps entrepreneurs build a "sales ministry" that listens to customers.

The language of "evangelist" is especially prevalent in the world of e-commerce. E-CEOs use the word *evangelize* a lot. Tom Jermoluk is chair and CEO of @Home Network *(www.home.net)*, a Silicon Valley firm that has exclusive rights to provide Internet access to AT&T's cable system. Jermoluk ("TJ" to his colleagues) estimates that "at least 50% of my job is being an evangelist—with our employees, the Street, the press, my partners." Remarks John Chambers, CEO of Cisco Systems *(www.cisco.com)*, "'Evangelizing?' I spend way more than half my time on that." Unlike most e-CEOs, he runs a long-established, hugely profitable company. Yet even he has to keep flagging the vision of the vast scope of the Internet revolution. "You've got to evangelize the concept," he says.[36]

The ultimate irony and indictment for the Christian community is to learn that the key professions for the future are the following: healers, peacemakers, storytellers, content providers. Are these not key words of our mission? Why aren't Christians at the forefront of building this new world?

† † †

They have . . . eyes, but do not see.
They have ears, but do not hear;
noses, but do not smell.
They have hands, but do not feel.

—Psalm 115:5–7 (NRSV)

† † †

Sensible Worship

In postmodern culture, there is no interest in a "second-hand" God, a God that someone else (church tradition, church professionals, church bureaucracies) defines for us. Each one of us is a Jacob become Israel: a wrestler with God. The encounter, the experience *is* the message.

Postmoderns literally "feel" their way through life. Want to create change? Give postmoderns a new experience they haven't had before. The experience of a new story, the "feel" of a new consciousness, is the key to personal and social change. "The language of God," John of the Cross once said, "is the experience of God written into our lives."

If postmodern worship can't make people furiously *feel* and *think* (in the modern world the church made people only "think"), it can't show them how God's Word transforms the way we "feel."

Total Experience is the new watchword in postmodern worship. New World preachers don't "write sermons." They create total experiences.[37] And these *Shekhinah* experiences (*Shekhinah* is the Hebrew term for the divine presence) bring together the full panoply of senses—sound, sight, touch, taste, and smell—into a radiant glowing of God's presence dwelling with God's people suffused in the ethereal light of beauty, truth, and goodness. Even classical music is becoming multimedial and multisensory to attract postmoderns. If the Portland Opera can pass out "scratch and sniff" cards to help its patrons follow the action on stage,[38] perhaps the church should re-learn how to swing its own thurible (incense boat).

It will not be easy for Protestantism to make this transition to worship that meets the "wow" standard. As much as the modern university, the modern church is the intellectual outgrowth of the Enlightenment, which tried to make the critical use of reason, not experience, the touchstone of knowledge. Jane Miller recalls her experience at Cambridge in the mid-twentieth century: "I have to admit, I believed you should not include anything you actually thought or felt in an essay."[39] We are now living in a world where one author, in his preface to a management text on leadership, declares defiantly: "I am not interested in appealing to anyone's rational mind, to inform or persuade, but to evoke their wild heart of ecstatic love."[40]

In this New World, you don't have to explain everything. Unlike Enlightenment culture, where everything had to "make sense," postmoderns luxuriate in mystery. Best-selling author Kathleen Norris tells of her own experience with modern churches that tried to chase all shadows into the rationalist light:

> The churches, like the liberal Protestant church I was raised in, don't want to talk about mystery. Of course when you are dealing with the Christian religion, it gets pretty comical because you either have to try to explain away the mysteries and miracles that are in Scripture and in the tradition, or you have to ignore them. I think there is a lot of both going on. Ironically one of the appeals that the Catholic church has these days, and the Episcopal church to some extent, is that they don't shortchange mystery. They are willing to talk about it. They don't try to explain everything away, don't try to talk everything through. That's a remarkable and freeing thinking.[41]

The triumph of Enlightenment[42] rationalism in worship is demonstrated in the statistics of a 1998 Barna Research Group study, which found that 32 percent of all stripes of regular churchgoers have *never* experienced God's presence in worship. Forty-four percent have not experienced God's presence in the past year (1997).[43] And the younger you are, the less likely you are to have a religious experience in worship. As appalling as these figures are, the percentages would be even higher if mainline Protestants were isolated out for comparison.

The degree to which we are captives of print and page was made clear at a gathering of Washington Presbyterians. I watched in amazement as the entire congregation of seven hundred people obediently followed the instructions in the bulletin, turned to the page for the black spiritual "Amen, Amen," and read from their hymnbooks, with heads bowed and legs braced, the one-word song: "A-men, A-men, A-men, A-men, A-men."

Idolic

Postmoderns have replaced the work ethic with an experience ethic. They value nothing higher than accumulated experience and will sacrifice everything for it, including committed relationships. Not just a can of worms, then, but a whole tub of worms is opened up by this experience ethic. Experiences can become idolic as well as addictive. Postmoderns collect "experiences" like moderns collected "stuff."

To a culture that more readily worships its spiritual experiences than the subject of its experiences, there is the Book of Hebrews, an antidote to postmodern feelingism. Experience is not the final arbiter of truth. Experience cannot be trusted except it has been transfigured by Scripture and Tradition. Besides, there comes a time when it's not time for experiences, but for obedience. It is up to the church to offer the Cyber Age Christ-initiated, biblically generated experiences.[44]

The Harvard philosopher Robert Nozick uses an experiential thought experiment to animate the dangers in experiential economies:

> Suppose there were an experience machine that would give you any experience you desired . . . you would think and feel you were writing a great novel, or making a friend, or reading an interesting book. All the time you would be floating in a tank, with electrodes attached to your brain . . . Would you plug in? What else can matter to us, other than how our lives feel from the inside?

Nozick answers his own question by declaring three objections: we want to do certain things, not just "experience" them; we want to be a certain sort of person; and we want contact with reality, "not just with the experience of reality."[45]

Christians must say yes to the moment God has given them. And the postmodern moment is a more experiential than rational moment. But saying yes to the moment does not mean one lets the moment define the yes.

I have dedicated my ministry to moving the church back to the future—in England this is called "radical orthodoxy,"[46] in New Zealand and Australia "alternative worship,"[47] in North America "ancientfuture faith."[48] I plead guilty, and am guilty, of being a man of his time. We are all time travelers. Even Jesus existed in time.

The question I have had to face in my own ministry is this: Will I live the time God has given me? Or will I live a time I would prefer to have? Postmodern culture is my here and now. I will take the church back to the cyberage, or will perish in the attempt. I live my life between two metaphors: (1) the pioneer who has arrows in his back, and (2) the slow buffalo always gets shot.[49] I am constantly aware that the difference between a leader and a martyr is about three paces.

† † †

There's . . . nothing you can do,
  but you can learn how to be you in time.
                                        —John Lennon lyric[50]

† † †

I yield to no one in helping the church move back to the future, in believing that good things can happen once again in our churches, in believing that the best days for my own Wesleyan tribe are in the future.

But . . . .

We aren't called to preach the times. We are called to preach eternities *to* the times. Jacob Bronowski called the principle that binds society together, in science as well as outside, "the principle of truthfulness." The church infects the culture with truths, not trends. The church must not come down with the "trendies." A deadly disease, this affliction called "trendinitis." Not just because Christians must choose the heftier over the trendier, but mostly because "trendinitis" misdiagnoses what is going on out there. We are living in a world where there are no more trends. Nothing is staying put or still long enough to become a trend. What's going on out there is terminally hip.

There is a difference between trailblazing and trendsetting. There is a difference between the spirit of newness and the spirit of nowness. The *Geist* in our *Zeit* must be the Heilige Geist. The spirit of *our* times must be the Holy Spirit.

Leaders do not strive to replace the "modern consciousness" with a "postmodern consciousness." Leaders help replace the "modern consciousness" with a "Christ consciousness" that can live and move and have its being in postmodern culture. If you remember nothing else in this book, remember this call for the church to recover tradition. We can become a "traditional" church by nurturing a culture that is identifiably Christian and postmodern at the same time, not one that looks like postmodern culture itself. The EPIC church carries the brand of the past while being a barometer of the future.

In my computer file I abbreviate "postmodern" with "po mo." My notes for this read "no po mo." We must be able to say no to "po mo." I had a parishioner once who never just said no. When she said no, she would say this, "Are you kidding? Not just no. But _____ no." Or as our kids put it today, "What part of NO don't you understand?"

There are certain presuppositions in the postmodern worldview that are opposed to the Christian worldview as revealed in the biblical texts and traditions of our faith. I want us to become not worldly wise but worldly unwise.

✝ ✝ ✝

Christ does not give Himself the name "Custom" but "Truth."

—Augustine

✝ ✝ ✝

God's everlasting yes has been sounded in Jesus Christ. But God's everlasting no has been sounded against all false values and loyalties—whether to Baal or Caesar—Bora Bora or Coca-Cola.

Welsh priest-poet R. S. Thomas, when out walking in the countryside of Wales, has a custom of "putting his hand in the place where a hare has recently lain, hoping to find it still warm."[51]

Postmoderns are constantly putting their hands and the rest of their bodies as well where God may have visited, hoping it's still warm. They are hungry for experiences, especially experiences of God.

Faith Practices and Web Interactives

1. Rent the romance movie *Simply Irresistible.* All of chef Amanda Cheldon's feelings went into her food. She gave her customers an experience with every course—an experience of sadness with the soup, silence with the salad, laughter with the main course, and romance with the desert. Do you agree that postmoderns want to experience all the extremes of emotion, even in their food. Note how he kept saying, "I think . . ." while she kept countering, "How do you feel?"

Or rent *Babette's Feast* and ask some of the same questions.

2. Church consultant Bill Easum has estimated that three out of four established churches will close in the next thirty years unless they transition into doing church differently.[52] Those most vulnerable? With attendance of eighty to two hundred.

Do you agree? How would you counter and challenge Easum's predictions?

3. Have you noticed the public-service campaign of messages from "God" displayed on billboards and bus shelters? The anonymous donor hired an ad agency to "remind people of God, especially people who used to go to church and for some reason don't go anymore, which is a good-sized group."[53] Discuss why it is ad agencies and anonymous donors are doing what the church should be doing. Discuss also how much of a "paraphrase" it is to change the biblical texts to the following "messages":

"That 'Love thy neighbor' thing. I mean it."

"Will the road you're on get you to my place?"

"Have you read my number-one best-seller? There will be a test."

"Loved the wedding. Invite me to the marriage."

"I don't question your existence."

"Keep using my name in vain, and I'll make rush hours longer."

"We need to talk." God

4. Someone once asked, "I wonder what the saints talk about in glory?" Then he answered his own question:

Perhaps one of their themes is this: Paul probably talks about his encounter with God on the Damascus Road. The Samaritan woman probably talks about her experience with the permanent water at the well. Zaccheus probably talks about his exchange with God while he was up a tree. Peter probably mentions his denial but then joyfully speaks of his encounter with the God of forgiveness. But to be sure, they all say, "There, God met me!"[54]

Where were you apprehended by an experience of the risen Christ?

5. Check out the "Xperiences" section of one of the most eye-popping sites on the Web dedicated to youth and college age students: *http://www.phatphish.com*. How are postmodern "Xperiences" different from what the modern world called "testimonials"?

6. *http://www.godscounter.com*. A portal to different Christian sites online. Assess and compare their mission statement with another similar site: *www.jesusnet.net*.

7. What ancientfuture components can you find in *http://www.ptcc.org*.

8. More and more people are selecting churches on the basis of music. One of the surprise findings of the 1994 Louisville Institute Conference on "Baby Boomers and the Changing Shape of American Religion" was that the most effective way to attract boomers was "expressive music—music that touches the heart." Number 2? Preaching and the pastor. Number 3? "Experiential dimension" of worship. Almost nonexistent was denominational linkages.[55]

How does your church compare with these statistics?

9. "Neither a wise man nor a brave man lies down on the tracks of history to wait for the train of the future to run over him," said President Dwight David Eisenhower.

The train is coming. Discuss what that train looks like from your angle of vision. Are you or your church on the tracks?

✓ 10. Check out *www.burningman.com,* the "burning man" experience. Why would people spend $100 a ticket to be part of this "experience"? How is this EPIC?

11. In his call for a "two-winged" church—one wing for celebration, the other wing for cells (small-group community), William A. Beckham warns that a one-winged bird can't fly.

> Some churches, after researching what the contemporary generation wants, are trying to give them the experience they demand. The strategy is to package the church in a new way so that members get more experience and less knowledge. However, without a New Testament small group of transparent fellowship, the church will be no more successful on the experience side than it was on the knowledge side.[56]

Is your church stronger in one wing or another? Is its cell wing stronger than its celebration wing? Or vice versa?

12. What do you think Dietrich Bonhoeffer meant when he said, "We are bound together by faith, not by experience."[57]

✝ ✝ ✝

Chapter Two

E-P-I-C Church for Epic Times

E-P(articipatory)-I-C

eBay

The eBay auction site, which gets twenty million hits a day, has been called a "participant sport." I felt the competitive juices flow and adrenaline rush in the midst of a weeklong bidding war over an 1827 pewter communion token. eBay has made me into a global buyer and seller—of books, Christian artifacts, art, and antiques.

At eBay the power belongs to the people, not to the producers.

In the world of e-commerce, the buyer sets the price. There is no more "price list." There is only what the customer is willing to pay for it. In the "auction economy" of eBay, the customer is king! It's the medieval bazaar come back to life in cyberspace.

Some call this haggling the "age of participation."[1] Others call it the "horizontal society."[2] Postmodern people take cues not from those "above" them but from others "around" them. There are no more bosses, only clients. In this radical democracy, vertical authorities like priests and professors have been replaced by peers throughout the world who share common interests.

Everything fixed is becoming fluid. It is not only the center that can't hold. The vertical can't hold either. It is not just that we're all priests. We're all doctors; we're all lawyers;[3] we're all architects; we're all programmers;[4] we're all stockbrokers;[5] we're all gourmets;[6] we're all philosophers (so says John Paul II in *Fides et Ratio*); we're all literary critics.[7] Now we're even all actors (who pay to be a part of Civil War battle reenactments).

Postmoderns are thinking and living within an interdependent, interactive ethos. They perceive, comprehend, and interact with the world as much as participants as observers.

After the U.S. Women's World Cup team victory over China, a *USA Today* editorial mused as to why sponsorship and salaries of soccer did not match that of sports like football and basketball: "If soccer does break through, it may well be measured by a different type of success: Not number of viewers, but number of participants."[8] In the next twenty years a sports game will be invented in which the audience becomes part of the competition itself (World Wide Wrestling doesn't count).

In 1997, four hundred thousand votes were cast in Nickelodeon's "Kids Choice Awards." One year later in 1998, that number increased to 4.5 million.

We're all authorities in whatever we're doing. Even kids. The Web makes everyone into a "content provider"—author, publisher, broadcaster, artist, expert.

KARAOKE CULTURE

Egil is our youngest child. One of his favorite toys is a Fischer-Price radio that comes with a karaoke unit. It isn't "music" unless he can perform and participate in it himself.[9]

Karaoke is a word that is now in the *New Shorter Oxford English Dictionary*, the world's first computer-generated dictionary. We hear the sounds of a karaoke culture in the phrase, "Talk to me." We hear the sounds of a karaoke culture in talk radio. One of every six USAmericans is a regular listener to talk radio.[10]

Mouse potatoes and click potatoes don't become couch potatoes. They become karaoke mike holders—or scuba divers, in-line skaters, mountain bikers, windsurfers.[11] The real content of medialike phones is not the information but the interaction.

This is the "value" of media that people in the church have yet to understand. The true content of multimedia is interaction. The key to all computer games[12] is interactive participation. And this interaction is what helps to create the experience we talked about in chapter 1. Sorbonne Professor Anne-Marie Duguet, head of the Centre de Recherches d'Esthétique du Cinéma et des Arts Audiovisuels, defines the creators of interactive arts as the "authors of experience."

That's why the more digital the culture becomes, the more participatory it gets. In 1994 NBC plunged from the tops of its skyscraper to the streets and made the passerby part of its morning *Today* show. By 1999, CBS and ABC had not just redesigned themselves to be street-level in their morning consciousness. They had fallen from the heights to be street-level in their participation as well.

The notion that electronic culture produces "couch potatoes" has pockmarked the mind of the church for too long. The truth is just the opposite. Electronic culture pushes postmoderns toward more active and interactive behaviors.

"Connexity Kids"

"Connexity Kids" and "Net Gens" are phrases used to describe our youngest generations. The marketing firm Saatchi & Saatchi invented the phrase "connexity kids" to convey the ways in which kids go "through the screen" in their interaction with life. In the words of Myra Stark, a senior vice president and director of knowledge management with Saatchi's New York office, "At first they're on the outside looking in, fascinated. Once they go through the screen, it's integrated into their lives."[13]

Postmoderns exhibit three levels of engagement with media (with life itself?), according to Stark: "fascination, exploration, integration." Postmoderns have to explore (hands-on) before they can integrate. Of these three stages, only the first is passive (fascination).[14] Both exploration and integration are active and interactive.

In other words, interactivity is hard-wired into the postmodern brain itself. This is the key to cyberspace: it is an interactive form of communication, a two-way media. Print, radio, TV, all are one-way. The cyberspace of phone and Web are by nature two-way communication.

The more you surf the Internet, the more you become "surf bored," as Jim L. Wilson puts it,[15] and want to surf the real thing. Have you noticed how kids can't sit still and listen to a concert? They make concerts interactive. At rock concerts there is slam dancing, mashing, even "bodysurfing" where people get "passed" overhead during the singing in about as "hands-on" a form of interactivity as one can invent.

† † †

> *In some strange sense, this is a participatory universe.*
> —Physicist John Wheeler

† † †

Of course, there is nothing new about the interactivity of children. According to Barbara Hayes-Roth of Stanford's Knowledge Systems Laboratory, every parent has had the experience of a child's shaping a story into recognizable form and exerting some control over the plot line. The parent begins: "Once upon a time, there was a rabbit."
"His name was Thomas!" says the child (whose name happens to be Thomas).

"Yes, his name was Thomas. And he lived in a burrow—"
"In a field? Was it in a field?"
"A big green field. And he had a friend—do you know what the friend's name was."
"Um—Samantha!"

"All right. One day, Thomas and Samantha went to gather blackberries."

"But rabbits don't eat blackberries. Rabbits eat grass."

"Most rabbits eat grass, but these were special rabbits."

The story becomes the by-product of the interactive creativity of both parent and child. Hayes-Roth points out that this is the exact process that brought to life *Alice in Wonderland*. This book was originally developed by Charles Lutwidge Dodgson (aka Lewis Carroll) telling stories to three schoolgirls, getting the Liddell sisters to ask questions and raise issues, and then their making requests that were then adopted. In other words, here is a book that emerged from interactivity.[16]

What is different about today's form of interactivity is that postmoderns have affixed a karaoke handle to everything. If there is no karaoke handle, they won't touch it. Cars that can be customized were a $19 billion market in 1997.[17] In the near future, there will be virtually no cars sold that haven't been personally customized.

A little mouthful of participation is not enough. Postmodern interactivity changes the menu itself. The restaurants of the future are those where you mix and match from the menu ("substitutions" are a small step in this direction), or better yet, tell the chef what you want to eat, and the waiter sets a personalized table filled with food that fits your diet, budget, tastes, and occasion.

Postmoderns are not simply going to transmit the tradition or the culture they've been taught. They won't take it unless they can transform it and customize it. Making a culture their own doesn't mean passing on a treasure that they've inherited, but inventing and engineering their own heirloom out of the treasures of the past. The Net enables them to do that.

Too often interactivity is like checking out of a motel room: once you leave, no one would ever have known you were there. True interactivity is not just that you can fool with something and find out how it works but that you can somehow change its workings. And the change is such that when you leave it there is evidence you were there. In the words of interactive experience designer Edwin Schlossberg, "A rich interactive experience is a game, like chess or Monopoly, in which the outcome of each move affects the overall experience."[18]

My dream Web site is a Linux interaction where anyone who visits the site can change it any way they think makes it better. An example of interactive participation that changes the character of the experience?

The Rhode Island gift shop OOP is just down the street from Brown University and RISDE in Providence. The owners get customer feedback by offering them $5 gift certificates and then uses their comments on tissue paper which is then used to wrap gifts. The wrapping paper you take home with you has such comments as "The men who work here are so cute" or "I don't need any of this stuff, but I want it" or "I used to have one of those when I was a kid."

From Representative to Participatory

A representative culture is based on certain beliefs:[19]
- People want and need to be controlled and have decisions made for them.

- The task of leadership is to administer guidance and regulations.
- People do only the things they are rewarded for doing.
- People cannot be trusted to use their personal freedom in service of the society or organization.

A participatory culture is based on just the opposite beliefs:

- People want to make their own decisions and have multiple choices.
- Leadership is emboldening and empowering others to lead.
- People will make sacrifices for the good of the whole.
- Human systems are self-organizing, and people can be trusted to invest wisely of their resources and time.

Here's a conversation overheard in a restaurant:

"Give me a Coke."

"Would you like a Classic Coke, a New Coke, a Cherry Coke, or a Diet Coke?"

"I'd like a Diet Coke."

"Would you like a regular Diet Coke or a caffeine-free Diet Coke?"

"Forget it. Give me a 7-Up."[20]

Postmodern culture is a choice culture. At the rocky hill in Athens called the "Areopagus," there was installed an altar inscribed to an "Unknown God" (Acts 17:23). The people of Athens were not unlike postmoderns. They wanted to keep their options open. It was Paul's job to introduce the wise Athenians to this "unknown God" in ways that they could hear and believe. To do this he had to participate in their culture, quote their poets, and establish common ground with them.

Whether first-century Athens or twenty-first century North America, a choice culture is by definition a participatory culture. And postmodern culture is becoming more participatory as it becomes: (1) more invasive (pacemakers, organ transplants, prosthetics), (2) more extrusive (video-conferencing, on-line education), and (3) more immersive (computer games, simulation rides, virtual reality).

Postmoderns don't give their undivided attention to much of anything without its being interactive. It is no longer enough to possess things or to enjoy positive events. One now has to be involved in bringing those events to pass or brokering those things into the home. People want to participate in the production of content, whatever it is. One reason why democracy has triumphed around the world is partly because of its interactivity: it is the most interactive model of government ever invented. But even democracy itself must shift from representative democracy to participatory democracy if it is to survive in the future.

The cultural shift from passivity to interactivity is the biggest reason for the decreasing popularity of television in postmodern culture. The finale of *Seinfeld* attracted 76.3 million viewers in 1998. The finale of *Cheers* attracted 80.5 million viewers in 1993. The finale of *M*A*S*H* attracted 106 million viewers in 1983. That's a drop of 30 million viewers while during the same time the total number of television households grew by 16 million.[21] Among children ages 3 through 12 especially, TV watching plummeted between 1981 and 1997, now stuck at 90 minutes a day during the week and two-and-a-half hours on weekends.[22]

Why? TV isn't nearly interactive enough. In the words of Steve Jobs of Apple Computers, "You go to your TV when you want to turn your brain off. You go to your computer when you want to turn your brain on." With a wired universe, each person can be a programmer, not just an observer. Television news has a stable audience only among those fifty or older. Everyone else is getting their information elsewhere. In fact, it's hard to find a successful new television program without an interactive component: from calling in your guilty or not guilty verdict, to the Emmy's featuring Internet polls that vote for the most memorable moments on television that past year. No wonder interactivity is the central focus of content providers.

Why is Margaret Wise Brown's *Good Night Moon* such a classic? It's totally interactive. My millennial kids Thane, Soren, and Egil are being brought up on interactive books like *Good Night Moon* and interactive games like *Just Grandma and Me, Arthur's Teacher Trouble, Reader Rabbit, Where in the World is Carmen Sandiago?* and other exercises in interfiction where the passivity of the printed word is blown apart. The Robin and Rand Miller CD-ROM game *Myst* is as much a classic in its own genre as James Joyce's *Ulysses* is in literature. On-line interactive story spaces are transitioning us into virtual reality environments of the future.

My four-year-old daughter Soren has no idea who Bert and Ernie are. Or Big Bird or Oscar, for that matter. *Sesame Street* has lost millions of kids because it didn't understand the shift from representation to participation. An interactive *Sesame Street* is now being prepared that will run on WebTV. Too little too late for my Soren.

The handwriting is already on the screen wall. For the first time ever, in 1999 videogames outperformed domestic box office movies in gross income.[23] Why? *GoldenEye* (Nintendo) is highly interactive. *GoldenEye* (MGM/UA) was not interactive at all.

† † †

Knowledge is both objective and participatory.
                              —Chemist Ilya Prigogine

† † †

Weddings

Even adults are making rituals of marriage and remembrance more EPIC. Instead of hiring expensive professional photographers, more and more wedding receptions have cameras scattered at tables with the invitation for the guests to take pictures. Couples increasingly are presenting to each other symbols of the things they bring to their union.

Instead of clinking glasses at wedding receptions, there are tables singing love songs to the bride and groom, pull-the-kiss-from-the-hat performances,[24] and the surrender of the keys.[25]

Funerals

At the same time the three largest funeral companies bury one in four USAmericans, do-it-yourself funerals are at record highs. More and more of us are bypassing funeral homes and burying our dead without mortuaries, cemeteries, or embalming.[26] Al Carpenter owns a no-frills mortuary in Alameda, California, that specializes in homemade caskets.

His eight-page guide entitled "How to Build Your Own Caskets" gets people involved in their own death process in new ways and even gives suggestions for what you can do with your casket while it is not being used:

- Attach legs and use as a coffee table.
- Toy chest or hope chest.
- Install shelves and use as a bookcase or hutch.

More participatory memorial rites and rituals are being created by postmoderns alongside the more "official" and representative rituals. The recent slate of high-school slaughterings introduced ad hoc shrines, white caskets that mourners can sign, individual urns for the mourners to take some of the deceased's ashes home with them, and eulogies in which almost everyone present has got to say something.

Pastors who have buried teenagers in the last ten years tell of their unwillingness to leave the viewing until they have written a note to the deceased and dropped it in the casket. After Steven Curtis Chapman finished singing at his high school alma mater, where three kids had been killed by one of their classmates, the kids piled out of their seats at the Paducah, Kentucky, memorial service and signed the three caskets. Same with Littleton, Colorado. The demand is so high that you can now purchase white signature caskets expressly for this reason.

Why the phenomenal growth of Mormonism? You can't be a Mormon and not go to church on Sunday morning. You wear certain clothing. You dedicate certain years of your life to mission work. You take pilgrimages to various meccas (Palmyra, Salt Lake City, etc.). Even when you die, there are rituals that must be conducted on the body by the family and by no one else.

Medicine

One of the mysteries of life is why anyone would use an electric toothbrush. I have a theory. These worthless instruments turn the person who uses them into a dentist—a pain-free dentist at that.

In medicine, we used to have three options: preventative, palliative, and curative. Now there is a fourth option: substitutive, where body parts or functions can be substituted. What is common to all four options, however, is this: all options now depend on the participation of the patient. There are no more authoritarian doctors and passive-active patients. According to the chair and CEO of Medtronics, "The real revolution taking place in this country is not managed care, but instead it is patient power. Patients are taking control of their own health care, really for the first time."[27]

The "Mayo Experience" at Rochester, Minnesota's Mayo Clinic (founded in 1889) features "total teamwork" to the level of an art form. To facilitate the team model, all the physicians earn a set salary. They address one another as "consultants" and storm every patient's problems as an integrated team. Mayo patients are at the heart of the team. In the words of one of the administrators, Dr. Lynn Hartman:

> Patients have shown over the past decade that they want to become active participants in their care. . . . They're on the Internet; they're doing their own research. By the time we see them, they're often fortified by an impressive body of information. What they're looking for is someone who can help them sort through that information. . . . Most patients today want a more interactive style, so that they can be part of the decision.[28]

Music

In music, and indeed all the arts, the major push is toward greater levels of participation and to draw you into a relationship with the art. Not many are as radical about getting the viewer to interact with the art in some way as composer and Zen practitioner John Cage. Cage is opposed to records, refuses to have any electronic recording equipment in his home, and recommends that "the more records you break, the more music you will have. Because ultimately you'll be obliged to sing yourself."[29] More commonplace are contemporary composers like David Lumsdaine. He writes music that can be listened to in a nonlinear fashion, music that is composed in such a way that everyone really makes their own composition out of it.[30]

On *www.tunes.com,* music fans can write their own reviews and post to message boards, with pop-up recommendations from the site and the fans on each page. Music producer and manager Linda Goldstein arranged a tour for singer Bobby McFerrin in which local choirs and whole audiences participate in the performance. And everyone styles themselves a musician. In the words of one author, "I am agnostic and have no remarkable musical ability, but I am auditioning for a spot in a semiprofessional chorale dedicated to sacred classical music."[31]

Economics

Postmoderns are often misunderstood as "it's all about me." Actually, it's less about "me, me, me" than about participation, participation, participation. People want to live within their own experience, not the experience of what they read or see. They want to experience it for themselves and help create what they experience.

Individuality is not being different so much as it is being oneself. The "democratization of creativity" means that participation is customized at every exchange and interchange. Delia's has an on-line store *(www.dELiAs.com)* that encourages buyers to mix and match to create their own look. The assumption is that every user is a clothing designer.

Businesses will do anything to get kids and "adult teens" to participate. According to Marketing Pulse, interactive ads engender up to 89 percent viewer participation and boost sales 21 percent.[32] At the Web sites for Auto-By-Tel *(www.autobytel.com)* or CarPoint *(www.carpoint.com),* you can buy a car on-line and specify every detail right down to the trim on the steering wheel. Customer specifications drive what is built.

The future of marketing in a do-it-yourself culture is not in selling an image or a brand but in making it possible for people to design and customize everything for themselves. The use of "real teens" rather than "professionals" as models in magazines (Levi's jeans, Skechers shoes, etc.) will only become more ubiquitous. In the future, people will get paid to visit ads rather than companies paying other companies to advertise. Yoyodyne already does what they call "permission-based marketing" as opposed to "interruption-based marketing." Customers themselves will be valued as the best consultants any company can have. The Web's participatory environment enables people outside the company to help design products and ponder procedures inside the company—be that company cars, clothes, drugs, or soft drinks.

EDUCATION

Philip Bigler is a public school teacher at Thomas Jefferson High School (Fairfax County, Virginia). In 1998, he was named Teacher of the Year. In his acceptance speech he spoke eloquently of the changes in learning from modern to postmodern:

> You can't be an effective teacher unless you're a constant learner. One thing that was the most difficult for me to unlearn was how to teach. Teachers are no longer the sage on the stage, imparting knowledge to a group of passive kids. To be effective now, I don't have to be "the authority." Rather, I need to let kids explore learning themselves. I might see a quicker way of getting from point A to point B, but the knowledge that kids gain is fundamentally richer when they get there on their own.
>
> I used to try to control my students' learning by insisting on certain processes. For instance, I would require students to show me note cards on their research papers. It was how I checked up on their work—and how I made sure that they were doing it my way. Then, one day, a group of students refused to do it my way; it just wasn't how they did things. I had failed to understand those kids' natural motivation and creativity. Now I can accept and appreciate that students' products are their answers, not their processes.[33]

Because of the dearth of public school teachers like Philip Bigler, we are faced with the hypocrisy of drug-free zones being turned into drug-dealing districts. School nurses spend their days dispensing psychostimulants with pharmacological effects almost indistinguishable from those of cocaine[34] because this culture finds it easier to drug its children into lecture-drill-test learning than to change its teaching methods to fit the EPIC learning styles of postmodern generations. Ritalin is now used by more than 4 million

USAmerican children, with four times as many boys as girls diagnosed as ADD, the most commonly diagnosed child psychiatric disorder in the US.[35]

The irony is that museums are now more EPIC than our public classrooms. In 1988, the Brooklyn Children's Museum modeled an interactive exhibit on cultural and scientific topics called "The Mystery of Things." Actually, I grew up going to the Corning Glass Museum in Corning, New York, which pioneered an interactive, "hands-on" (they called it then) exhibit in 1951. The Minneapolis Institute of the Arts has devised six interactive exhibits since 1993. Some museums have taken the participatory and interactive to the limit: you can actually stay in them.[36]

Politics

Participation is materializing as the commanding form of governance systems. Participation is what brought down the Berlin Wall. Democracy is surging forward and cannot be stopped. There were sixty-nine countries called "democratic" in 1990. By 2000 there were 120.

It is only a matter of time before there will be such a thing as an "interactive jury." Can a jury ever be isolated and sequestered and silenced again after some of the high-profile trials of the 1990s? In the future outside contact will be encouraged, questions invited, and jurors' confusions about the law will be corrected at the start. Juries will take more charge of their own trials and participate in the process.

In the debate between "representative" and "participatory" democracy, the participatory side has won. The problem is no longer onerous taxation ("No taxation without representation"). The problem is now the lack of participation. ("No taxation without participation.") "Representation" simply doesn't do it anymore.

It is not clear whether an age of participation gives us more freedom or more meetings. This was Oscar Wilde's complaint about the burdens of some forms of government: "The trouble with socialism is that it does cut into one's evenings so dreadfully." The burdens of participatory democracy are even more demanding.

The Internet has put the participation back into participatory government. The Web has popped the cork, and there's no stopping it now.

Books

The greatest evidence and testimony to the participatory bent of postmodern culture is the world of books themselves. It used to be that "serious" books came without pictures or anything that would break up the print. As late as the early 1990s, when I wrote *Quantum Spirituality: A Postmodern Apologetic*,[37] a variety of publishers wanted to put the book under their masthead. Except they didn't want to break up the text with any of my interactive design components, back-lit pages, or text-bite insertions on the page. I ended up publishing the book myself rather than compromise on the merger of container and content.

Less than a decade later it is not uncommon to find interactive elements within traditional book formats.[38] In fact, there is now a word for it: "booktivity."[39] Eric Stanford, in his unpublished essay for authors, editors, and publishers entitled "Publishing for Postmoderns," explores why postmoderns like nonlinear approaches to presentation of the text. He believes it has something to do with more than the ways postmoderns approach and absorb information. He is convinced "the fundamental issue is one of power."

A nonlinear format represents an empowering of the reader, or more precisely, a shifting of power from the author to the reader. To read a traditional book is to sit under a teacher and passively take in whatever the teacher wants to tell you. To read a nonlinear book is to have some say in what the lecture covers or at least in how you will receive it.

The collage effect of nonlinear communication reflects postmodernism's radical democracy. Ideas and people are more or less equal, postmoderns believe. Nonlinearity puts the reader more nearly on a par with the author.[40]

RELiGiOn

After Pat Boone appeared in a heavy-metal outfit with his friend Alice Cooper (also a Christian) on the American Music Awards show, the Trinity Broadcasting Network did not just cancel his show, *Gospel America*. Paul Crouch asked Boone to appear with a panel of his peers on TBN's flagship talk show, *Praise the Lord*, to justify his actions and respond to his critics.

At the end of the broadcast, TBN viewers were asked to call in and vote whether or not Boone's show should return to the air. The calls came in overwhelmingly in favor of bringing back Boone's program. Although Boone is still not back on the air, *Christianity Today* is right in calling this interactive method of reconciling differences "a glimpse of what Christian television might look like if its purveyors were more willing to engage and grapple constructively with the world outside insulated church walls."[41]

Even newspapers are becoming more EPIC. Through bulletin boards and electronic mailboxes, staff can communicate with subscribers. If the most "We print it/You read it" organizations around are changing, "We preach it/You hear it" is over. Every congregation must become a participant-observer congregation.

The body of Christ is a participative community. Not just in the Eucharist is everyone a "participant," a part of the action, not apart from it. There are no more "professional clergy" and pew-sitting laity. There are only ministers who look to leaders to mobilize and release ministry through them. All "participants" are full partners.

What is the attractive power and mystery of Eastern Orthodox and neotraditional worship to postmoderns? It's the same as the attractive power and mystery of Pentecostalism—the fastest growing religious movement in the world.[42] Postmoderns want interactive, immersive, "in your face" participation in the mysteries of God. Pentecostals talk about "moving the service." To "move the service" is to facilitate intimacy with God through dance, speech, sound, touch, etc. To "move the service" is to transform anticipations into participations through interaction rituals.

Sometimes the Pentecostals and the neotraditionalists haven't only won; they've become one. For example, there is a fifteen-hundred-seat Pentecostal church in Valdosta, Georgia, which converted en masse to the Book of Common Prayer, with a bishop of the Episcopal Church carrying out the confirmation of the entire congregation on Good Friday, 1990. A whole charismatic movement in California joined the Orthodox Church, calling itself the Antiochian Orthodox Church.

Postmodern worship is body worship. Body piercings show postmodern desperation for rituals, including body rituals. Unlike moderns, whose body modification took the more invasive form of beauty-enhancing, age-defying plastic surgery, postmoderns are narrating the story of their lives on their bodies through multiple piercings (a dozen piercings are not uncommon). The role of spectacle in worship is only beginning to be understood.[43]

Ironically, it is the screen that releases postmoderns to "put their whole being" into worship and frees them from being chained in place by books. Sometimes the preaching will become more karaoke, other times more kinesthetic. But whatever form preaching takes, the interactive component is crucial. Unless postmoderns can complete the sentence for themselves, or at least have the opportunity to hold the mike themselves, worship will insufficiently help them create new realities for their lives.

Faced with a smorgasbord of choices, some people don't select one or the other. They select nothing at all. That's why the neotraditional movement will become stronger than it is now.

But while many couples want traditional weddings with all the trimmings, they want tradition "neo." "Neo" for them means tradition customized and personalized. Even neo-traditionalists make the tradition interactive. If they can't take tradition and run with it down their own path and journey, they won't pick it up.

† † †

I never think of my audiences as customers.
I think of them as partners.

—Actor Jimmy Stewart

† † †

Interactive preaching can be as simple as monitoring the reaction and resistance of your congregation with feedback loops like "I see some smiles" or "I feel some scowls out there." It can be as risky as what I call "karaoke preaching" where you stand out there in the midst of the congregation much like Phil Donahue started doing in the '70s, when he introduced the participatory talk show. Build a sermon together as you share your mike with them. Or it can be as safe as getting your congregation to finish your sentences for you (if they finish it, it's no longer your sentence; it's theirs). Musician/consultant Brian Eno says the word "unfinished" is better than "interactive." Whatever level of interaction you choose, there needs to be an interactive segue at least every eight minutes (which is three times people's visual attention span, now down to two or three minutes).

We need new names for worship experiences depending on their levels of interactivity. In the language of the pueblos (Tewa), everything has a different name, depending on its state of interactivity. For example, wood that is the trunk of a tree has a different name from wood burning in the fireplace, or wood legs on a chair, or wood leaves that are paper.

On Earth as It Is in Web Heaven

Teacher: "What's the nation's capital?"
Student: "Washington, D.C."
Teacher: "What does 'D.C.' stand for?"
Student: "Dot Com?"

The Internet is our kids' world. English is almost their second language. When Jack Welch, the CEO of GE, declares that the Internet is the biggest wave of change he has seen in his long career, he isn't saying the half of it. Kids are already playing interactive games on the Internet with kids from other countries, kids who don't even speak English. The Age of Empires is a game where students build their own personal empire and protect it from invaders. These are games that translate from Greek and Japanese into English automatically.

The level of disconnect between the world our kids are living in and the world of the church at times appears unbridgeable. There are a few bridge builders out there— leaders like Walt Kallstadt and Tim Wright of the "Community of Joy" in Phoenix, Arizona. Community Church of Joy *(www.joyonline.org)* is more than the largest Lutheran church in North America. It is one of today's more creative and innovative endeavors at offering postmoderns a transforming God experience.

Walt is acutely aware that the current system of fund-raising for the church, which is based on annual pledges supporting approved budgets, is increasingly inadequate for the postmodern world. Hence his introduction of "profit centers" within the Community of Joy. These are revenue-producing entities that both minister to people's needs while at the same time generating long-term income for the church's ministries.

During my recent tour of the Community of Joy, Walt showed me one of these "profit centers"—a columbarium. As I listened to him share his team's dreams for these memorial gardens, I thought of how ancient it all felt. Visit any church from the seventeenth or eighteenth century. What was usually next to it? A cemetery that the trustees of the church were often responsible for maintaining. Whenever I move to a new city, the first church I always visit is one that has a cemetery next to it. It's a way for me to connect with the communion of saints that are still a part of that community and a visual reminder of the theological truism that the majority of the church is underground. We live in covenant with them and continue their ministries.

I shared this with Walt but pressed him on the "participatory" component to Community of Joy as an EPIC Church. "Where's your on-line memorial garden?" I asked both impishly and seriously.

As For Me and My Mouse, We Will Serve the Lord

In postmodern culture memorialization has become quite complex. There used to be one body for the church to memorialize. In postmodern culture there are many bodies to be handled. And increasingly there will be many deaths (wetware death, software death, hardware death)—but that's another story.

Right now postmodern pastors must come to terms with multiple sites and with multiple rites and rituals of remembrance: specifically the real and the virtual. The real world already has multiple sites and rites at which we preside (church, home, "funeral home," cemetery). Where are you and your church ministering in the virtual world?

Of three kids still at home, only nine-year-old Thane has a memory of Gramma Sweet. Thane was three when his grandmother died, and one of our challenges is to keep his memories of his Gramma fresh and green. Whenever we hear him use a word he learned from his Gramma ("whoopsidaisy"), we remind him who taught him that word. We get out old family albums with pictures of the two of them together and tell "Gramma Sweet" stories that he then tells back to us.

But what if Thane could, whenever he missed his Gramma or wanted to talk to her, log on to a church Web site and have an angel personally escort him to Web heaven? There he could visit a memorial Web site, sponsored by the church and designed by Mabel Boggs Sweet and her three sons' families. It could feature among many other things:

- A page of Gramma's "favorites"—favorite Bible verses, favorite hymns (that Thane could click on and hear), favorite books, favorite places to visit, favorite quotes.
- Videos and photographs of his Gramma holding him and the other grandchildren—some candid shots, others specially intended just for Thane.
- A sermon given by this woman preacher/evangelist that her sons specially selected out of her repertoire.
- Some excerpts from her diary and commonplace book.
- Memorial messages from friends and family around the world who knew Gramma Sweet and whose lives were touched by her life and ministry.

With such an EPIC ministry, has the church increased the quality of its pastoral care or diminished it?

FAITH PRACTICES AND WEB INTERACTIVES

1. Check out Priceline.com or Travelocity.com. Can you find a "fixed" price anywhere?

2. Interactive game pioneer Walt Freitag, the founder of Daedalus Arts in Somerville, Massachusetts, says that storytelling and interactivity are mutually exclusive. He says that separating the two is "a pit of hell that can absorb endless amounts of time, skill, and resources."[44] He argues that a strong story line with all sorts of plot twists and surprises with a wow ending is not conducive to user interfacing. Vice versa, the rapture of freedom in an interactive world would be gone if a story line were to be forced on it.

Do you agree or disagree? Why?

3. Former seminary president Donald E. Messer tells a "true story emerging from World War II" which he offers as a "parable for our mission and ministry."

> Russian soldiers at the Rzhev front, working at night in freezing waters, built a secret bridge under the river's surface. When darkness covered the moon and snow shrouded the river, strong Russian swimmers silently worked chest-deep in the freezing waters. Their bodies were bloodied by the ice floes.
>
> Then one morning, to the utter shock of the Nazis, Russian tanks, whitened for winter war, came charging down the bank, crashed through the thin ice, and stormed across the river on the hidden bridge built beneath the water. Squadron after squadron roared across toward the stupefied Nazis, opening the Rzhev offensive.

Messer suggests that ministry in the twenty-first century needs to "construct bridges, not in order to assault others, but to create needed spans of understanding and communication. Perhaps we could even paraphrase Simon and Garfunkel and sing 'Bridge Under Troubled Waters'!"[45]

What are some of the hidden bridges your church is building into this new world? Is your church more of a bridge-builder or a bomb-thrower?

5. To encourage nonthreatening participation at funerals, Georgia Methodist W. Hamp Watson Jr. has prepared a Funeral Meditation Assistance Form with three component questions. People fill this out before the service and give it to the preacher. There are three questions, only one of which need be answered:

- When I remember _____, I think about . . .
- I remember when . . .
- I guess the most treasured experience I had with this loved one was when . . .

How would you finish these sentences about your grand-parents/parents?

6. Edwin Schlossburg, one of the world's leading designers of interactive learning, has written that "children, because of school, are now the only members of a local community who meet daily. As a result, aside from the sports audience, they have become the most marketable audience for programming on television. The objective of marketing is to create perceived value in an object. But perceived value only works as a currency in a community where the perception can be shared. Therefore, children at school every day fulfill both objectives. They can absorb the marketing and have a forum to show off their purchases."[46] How do you react to your children being manipulated in this way. What can be done to minimize it?

7. Check out WB network's *Dawson's Creek* Web site: *http://www.dawsons-creekcom/main.html*. Now browse the Web sites the fans have created (i.e., *ttp://hoflink.com/~tle/*).

Note the ways they are building community on-line.
"Fanfiction" is a new literary genre in which *Dawson's
Creek* "fans" can create their own plot lines around the television characters. In this way people participate in creating
the Dawson's Creek brand.[47]

8. Another example is Cartoon Network's Dexter's
Laboratory. For links to *Dexter's Laboratory,* check out
http://fn2.freenet.edmonton.ab.ca/~planet23/dexter.htm.
This is Paul Senior's Dexter Page. A competition advertised
on this site was won by an eight-year-old girl. She wrote an
episode of the show and appeared as her own cartoon character there.[48]

9. True or False? Wal-Mart, the world's biggest retailer,
got that way by seeing itself as buying for, not selling to, its
customers.

What are the implications of this switch for the church?

10. Check out the children's book section at a bookstore.
Note how kids are coauthoring their bedtime stories. Note
also the interactive features of the biggest sellers.

11. There are three key component strengths
("delights") to electronic interactivity, according to Janet
Murray: (a) immersion; (b) agency; (c) transformation.

- Immersion: The world of the screen transports you
  into another world and replicates you there to the nth
  degree, making it possible for you to do things you
  never thought you could do.

- Agency: Your agent does what you do and follows
  your instructions. "Agency is the satisfying power to
  take meaningful action and see the results of our decisions and choices."

- Transformation: Experience of fascination and wonder of playing with something that is virtual but in all respects real.[49]

Evaluate your interactive initiatives in ministry using these three criteria.

12. Discuss this thesis: The success of Habitat for Humanity is due in large part to its participatory structure. You get to do something personally; you get to know the people for whom you are doing it; and you get to give both money and time.

13. See if anyone remembers the ad where a guy is listening to a boring opera when his cell phone rings. He answers it and begins chatting. The diva, horrified by his impudence, takes her spear and hurls it toward him, striking a bull's-eye by piercing the cell phone and taking it out of his hands. He then starts inputting his words, the first ones of which are these: "Opera Just Got Interesting."

What does it take for church to "get interesting" to postmoderns? Is "interesting" an appropriate category for church?

14. In what way is participation different from teams? From "quality circles," or "focus groups?" From getting everyone involved in everything?

15. The University of Wisconsin at Madison authorized business students to invest $10 million of the school's endowment fund as part of their training. More and more colleges and universities are employing experiential, participatory methods of learning in the educational process. What risks is your church taking to help postmoderns come to terms with the claims of the gospel?

16. In your community which is doing better? PTOs or PTAs? What's the difference? PTA is a national bureaucracy

that boasts professionalized parent-teacher relationships. PTOs (Parent Teacher Organizations) are grassroots organizations that lobby for parents' participation in their children's education.[50]

17. Walk the candy aisles of K-mart or Wal-Mart and purchase a bunch of sample "interactive" candies. Remember those Atomic Balls? Tootsie Pops and Tootsie Rolls? How many do you see?

In their place are Glow Pops, Spin Pops, Big Bangs, Skull Suckers, Monster Mouths, Mega Warheads, Tongue Splashers.

Eat some.

These candies you experience and interact with come with warnings like "Eating multiple pieces within a short time period may cause a temporary irritation to sensitive tongues and mouths." They promise extreme flavor (super-sour, supersweet), extreme pleasure, extreme pain.

- Shock Tarts—"Feel the Power!"
- Nestle Nuclear Chocolate—"The explosive power of Pop Rocks popping candy"
- Nestle Armageddon Asteroid—"A smashable milk chocolate asteroid with intense meteorite candy inside"[51]

Talk to your kids about who they know who's a "warheads warlord"—a status of distinction earned by enduring flavors that explode in their mouths.

18. For a great example of a church Web site that has reinvented itself as an online magazine and fosters participation, see *www.bellview.org*.

19. Charles Arn makes it a principle that he's learned from personal observation and study: "The more unchurched your target audience, the more they will want to

listen to the music. The more churched your target audience, the more they will want to participate in it."[52]

And again: "The stronger the cultural identity of your target audience, the greater their desire for participation in the music. The weaker the cultural identity, the less desire for participation."[53]

Do you agree?

20. Check out "The Electronic Great Awakening" site *www.pcusa.org/ega,* a media literacy program sponsored by Presbyterians to help people understand and think critically about today's wired world. How should Christians respond to a media-saturated culture?[54]

21. Buy enough "Jones Soda Co." so that everyone can have their own bottle. (My favorite flavor—"Green Apple.") Read the label. What is Jones really selling? Notice any ancientfuture components? Why "Jones"? How powerful is their invitation to "send us your photo. If we like it we will put in on our label." For more, check out their Web site *www.jonessoda.com.*

22. Postmoderns are changing the very nature of philanthropy itself into more EPIC models. For the "venture philanthropy" movement which shuns passive models of giving money away and embraces more hands-on approaches to giving, check out Social Venture Partners *www.svpseattle.org* and The Entrepreneurs' Foundation *www.the-ef.org.* How might your church make its own fund-raising more participatory?

† † †

Chapter Three

Epic Church for Epic Times

E-P-I(mage-driven)-C

Experiential
Participatory

eBay

Visit as many of the more than two million eBay sites as you want. You'll find that almost every one has an image of what is for sale. Each image comes to life with story and sometimes music. Each site tries to bring you into a relationship with that image and story. And each one bears an image for the reputation of each seller and buyer.

eBay is not alone in using images to draw us into a relationship. NCR's ATM machines are "transforming transactions into relationships" according to their ads. Agency.com is dedicated to what it calls "interactive relationship management." Its slogan: "It's not the medium; it's the relationship."

The lesson for the church is simple: images generate emotions, and people will respond to their feelings.

Postmodern culture is image-driven. The modern world was word-based. Its theologians tried to create an intellectual faith, placing reason and order at the heart of religion. Mystery and metaphor were banished as too fuzzy, too mystical, too illogical. After forfeiting to the media the role of storyteller, the church now enters a world where story and metaphor are at the heart of spirituality.

Images come as close as human beings will get to a universal language. In the public school system of Fairfax County, Virginia, more than ninety different languages are spoken. But all of those ninety languages, and all the 6,500 languages of the world, share one common language: metaphor. Indeed, it seems clearer than ever that metaphysics is nothing but metaphor. Alter our metaphors, and we transform our being in the world. Alter our metaphors, and we are transformed into the image of Christ.

Propositions are lost on postmodern ears, but metaphor they will hear; images they will see and understand. Image dictionaries are replacing word dictionaries, and image banks are becoming as valuable as money banks (just ask Bill Gates). Cyberspace itself is becoming less word-based and more image-based through the spread of avatars (your self-crafted image on-line), which will be for our cyber life what our Social Security number is for our real life. As of this writing, avatars have at least seventeen actions and behaviors, including walking, waving, nodding yes and no, flying, flipping, twirling, etc.

Coca-Cola has become a global syrup, not by the touting of its ingredients or a competitive price, but by the conveyance of images and a ubiquitous logo. In fact, one senior Coca-Cola executive is said to have declared that the company could survive the loss of all its assets (plants, employees, even access to raw materials), providing it kept possession of the Coca-Cola logo. With that one image, he argued, it would be possible to walk into a bank and receive sufficient credit to replace Coke's entire global infrastructure.

If the biggest brands are those that "own stories" and the greatest resources anyone can "own" are images and stories, Christianity ought to be the biggest brand around. The church, not Hollywood, ought to be the world's greatest image factory.

The greatest image in the world, the image to which we draw people into a relationship, is the image of God in Jesus the Christ. Paul says of Jesus: "He is the image of the invisible God" (Col. 1:15 NRSV). Jesus says of himself: "If you know me, you will know my Father also. . . . Whoever has seen me has seen the Father" (John 14:7,9 NRSV).

† † †

The mind never thinks without a picture.

—Aristotle

† † †

GET THE PICTURE?

Cultures are symbol systems, intricate, interwoven webs of metaphors, symbols, and stories. What holds the culture of the church together—the metaphors it offers, the symbols it displays, the stories it tells? The postmodern church seems to have lost the plot to the "stories of Jesus." Could it be because the redemption story was told in the modern era more by "creeds" and "laws" than by "parables"—narrative-wrapped images?

A wonderfully strange, even crude, story circulated in the early church. It is best compared to a campfire story, when ancient Christian storytellers would give biblical narratives their own "spin" to help explain events that were happening in their own lives and to fill in the blanks in the biblical stories.

This folk story embellishes the biblical account of God's creating the heavens and the earth and everything in them through the use of words. "Let there be light," God said, and there was light.

"Let there be water. Let there be vegetation. Let there be animals. Let there be humans. Let it be done." And so it was done, because God's words were power.

It so happened, however, that the devil was jealous and angry about what God had done—especially the creation of those human creatures. Consequently, the devil tricked God into a confrontation. The devil asked him what was so special about these creatures Adam and Eve. When God opened his mouth to speak, the devil bound his tongue so that he could not talk. And since God's creative power was in his words, the devil had thwarted that power. As a result the devil pretty much had his way with human beings.

Aeons went by. But the devil couldn't resist coming back to mock God and gloat over his triumph. He began taunting the silent deity, and God responded by holding up one finger.

"One?" the devil asked. "Are you trying to tell me that you want to say just *one* word?"

God nodded in the affirmative, and the devil thought to himself, "I don't suppose that even God can do much harm to me with just one word." So the devil unbound God's tongue, and God spoke one word in a quiet whisper. It was a word that would resound forever in every corner of the universe. It was a word that represented total access to the kingdom of heaven for all God's children.

And the word God spoke was *Jesus!*

Fʀoᴍ Woʀᴅ-Bᴀsᴇᴅ ᴛo Ìᴍᴀɢᴇ-Dʀívᴇɴ

If you want people to think differently, Buckminster Fuller used to say, don't tell them how to think, give them a tool. The best tool religious leaders can give people to think and live differently is a metaphor or image.

Nietzsche was right: "We do not think good metaphors are anything very important, but I think a good metaphor is something even the police should keep an eye on."[1] Metaphors lodge truth in the imagination. In Emily Brontë's words about dreams, images go through one's life "like wine through water."[2]

To sculpt a metaphor is to create a world and transform the world.

Next time you are at the supermarket, ask the person at the fish counter for "fresh sardines." What happened? Were you embarrassed?

There is no fish named "sardine." The tin can may say "sardines." But the name applies to any of twenty-one species of small fish that, the moment they hit the tin, can be labeled "sardines."

You and I eat something all the time that doesn't exist. The metaphor of "sardine" is a construct to help us negotiate the complexity of twenty-one trash fish jammed into a can.

† † †

Nothing in law is so apt to mislead than a metaphor.
—Eighteenth-century English jurist Lord Mansfield

† † †

The danger comes when we no longer recognize something as a metaphor but see it as a literal truth. Idolatry is when you get stuck on the "sardine" to the point where the twenty-one-fish complexity is lost. Legal scholar-historian Bernard J. Hibbitts is wise in his warning that "paradoxically, the better a metaphor is, the worse this kind of problem threatens to become. In extreme circumstances, a good metaphor may be so compelling that it altogether subverts its referent's original meaning."[3] This is the forewarning of the first of the Ten Commandments, which tells us not to make images of God, even mental images.

There's a second double-edged danger with images. This danger is their fuzziness, which is both a strength and weakness. The fuzziness is what makes metaphors so user-friendly and accessible. Without sharp edges that cut and pierce, metaphors invite people to pick them up. But that very fuzziness can become a Rorschach inkblot that obscures even more than it illuminates.

And it can get us into deep trouble. I have ended up more than once in the wrong rest room in both Italian and Mexican restaurants because I carelessly looked at the images of Male and Female on the door and read them wrong. The words "Men" and "Women" are well-defined and easy to identify. The images for "Men" and "Women" are boundless and blurred.

Trimtab Effect

Buckminster Fuller tells about steering the course of "spaceship earth."

> I saw most people trying to turn the boat by pushing the bow around. I saw that by being all the way at the tail of the ship, by just kicking my foot to one side or the other, I could create the "low pressure" which would turn the whole ship. If ever someone wanted to write my epitaph, I would want it to say "Call me Trimtab."[4]

The trimtab effect occurs when one turns the tiny rudder on the trailing end of the main rudder. This enables the main rudder to turn the whole ship around with a lot less difficulty. The power of metaphor is the trimtab effect. Small changes in how we visualize life and the Spirit can generate massive changes in how we live our lives and configure our consciousness.

Visual language (metaphor evangelism, metaphor preaching, etc.) is no longer an option. We are a print-saturated, word-based church in the midst of visual technologies that are creating a whole new visual culture. This is one reason for the huge comeback of poetry. We are living in one of the golden ages of religious poetry (e.g., Welsh priest R. S. Thomas, Geoffrey Hill, Elizabeth Jennings, David Gascoyne, C. H. Sisson, and others). We may never return to the days when poet Roy Campbell got in a physical slugfest with poet Stephen Spender during a poetry reading at the South Place Ethical Church in Oxford. But we are living in a time when poetry contests are all the rage. Poetry contests used to be a highbrow activity in the eighteenth century. Now they're community contests where everyone participates.

Metaphors are the medium through which biblical spirituality will be fashioned for this new world. There are a variety of reasons why this is so.

† † †

The difference between the right word and the almost right word is the difference between lightning and a lightning bug.

—Mark Twain[5]

† † †

First, humans think in images, not words. In a visualholic culture like postmodernity it is difficult not to be persuaded by arguments like "the conceptual systems of cultures and religions are metaphorical in nature";[6] "the most fundamental values in a culture will be coherent with the metaphorical structure of the most fundamental concepts in the culture";[7] and that "concepts are not defined solely in terms of inherent properties; instead, they are defined primarily in terms of interactional properties."[8]

Image-driven is not distinctive to postmodern culture but to the human mind itself. The human mind is made up of metaphors. In defining realities, metaphors create realities. Metaphors are constitutive of both thought and action. Metaphors are more than matters of language.

> [Metaphor] is a matter of conceptual structure. And conceptual structure is not merely a matter of the intellect—it involves all the natural dimensions of our experience, including aspects of our sense experiences: color, shape, texture, sound, etc. These dimensions structure not only mundane experience but aesthetic experience as well.[9]

Metaphors are more than decorations. Metaphors are the most fundamental tools of thought. Metaphors are causes more than consequences of our reasoning. That's why the power of liturgy is so immense: liturgy realigns our metaphors to conform to Christ, which transforms our lives. Joseph Stalin was an ex-seminarian. From the Orthodox Church he learned the power of icons. That's why he littered the Soviet landscape with pictures of himself.

Icon-parables alter our perception of what is. Icon-parable storytelling helps us make decisions we need to make or reverse decisions we've already made. Without icon-parables, postmoderns are spiritually ill-fed. The first Christian icon was a textless symbol named ichthus (iota, chi, theta, upsilon, sigma)—a double-swoosh word symbol for fish.

As the single-swoosh Nike will testify, the ultimate in power is not to have the first position or the last word but to have the ability to order and ordain metaphors. In a postmodern culture, images operate as a language of power.

When I tell people that the only power I want is the power to choose and celebrate the metaphors, they shake their heads and say, "Sweet, you're too much." Instead of being afraid of such contra mundum designations, perhaps it's time leaders became willing to be "too much" in their use of metaphors. What did the religious establishment of Jesus' time find in this metaphor-wielding, parabolic preacher? Too much for them? Instead of hoping for honorary doctorates (D.D. degrees), perhaps Christians should be willing to embrace what the D.D. designation means in law enforcement lingo: "drunk and disorderly." The original disciples of Jesus were given this D.D. title: drunk with the Spirit and disorderly in turning the world upside down. We can keep up our contra mundums because of the metaphoric ministry of Jesus.

† † †

Way out people know the way out.
—Poet Bob Kaufman[10]

† † †

Second, postmodern spirituality is image-based. Postmodern culture is a double-ring culture,[11] and metaphors are themselves a double ring. Philosopher Max Black calls them "two ideas in one phrase" (e.g. sweet smile, sharp tongue, sour notes, etc.). Part of this pervasive both/and-ness comes from the shaping influence on postmodern thought of chaos theory and the complexity sciences (popularized by actor Jeff Goldblum in *Jurassic Park),* which look at the whole, the system, rather than dissect the parts. In searching for likenesses and similarities, complexity thinking invites metaphorical thinking and linking.

Third, worship is not about style; it's about spirit. This is
not to say that style is unimportant. You don't think style is
important? Tell VW Beetle that. You don't think style sells?
Tell that to Apple Computer. Their "Think Different" billboards and hood-shaped iMac computers that come in "flavors" (colors)—and now their clam-shaped laptop, the
iBook—are already studied in business schools as one of the
greatest turnaround stories of the twentieth century.

But if there is not the "right spirit," presentation means
little—no matter how contemporary or high-tech. Ten times
zero is still zero. If the spirit is there, presentation also means
little—no matter how traditional or bookish. Metaphors do
the heavy lifting. Metaphors generate a spirit that quickly
captures and charges space. That is why the Jesus method of
communication was not the exegesis of words but the exegesis of images: "the kingdom of heaven is like . . ."

Linda S. McCoy has planted a church called THE GAR-
DEN in Indianapolis, which meets in a Beef & Boards
Dinner Theater facility. The musical group The Good Earth
Band leads worshipers seated around tables through heavy
helpings of video clips, drama, secular music, and contemporary Christian music—keeping the service to forty minutes. A flowerpot at the door is the only offering plate.[12]

The importance of shifting worship from the exegesis of
words to the exegesis of images if we are to birth and build
churches that last was hammered home from studies of companies "built to last." Two Stanford Business School professors discovered to their surprise that the key to great
companies is not "visionary leadership" by some entrepre-
neurial CEO or a "big vision" of how best to command market share, but the creation of a web of shared meaning and

values around common metaphors that abide and guide the company into the future.[13]

✝ ✝ ✝

Words in the heart are not words.

—Talmud

✝ ✝ ✝

Metaphors function in society much like "imaginal cells" function in the body of a caterpillar on its way to becoming a butterfly. The metamorphosis from land to air begins when "imaginal cells" start forming in the caterpillar. These cells are the building blocks of the new organism which grows among and in between the old cells. As these "imaginal cells" prosper and emerge organically, the tissues of the old cells dissolve and disappear until all that is left is a butterfly.

The journal *Philosophy and Literature,* published by the University of Canterbury, in Christchurch, New Zealand, periodically gives Gold Medal awards in the Bad Writing Contest. One of the recent award winners was the distinguished scholar Fredric Jameson, whose opening sentence in *Signatures of the Visible* (1998) gives a portent of what follows:

> The visual is essentially pornographic, which is to say that it has its end in rapt, mindless fascination; thinking about its attributes becomes an adjunct to that, if it is unwilling to betray its object; while the most austere films necessarily draw their energy from the attempt to repress their own excess (rather than from the more thankless effort to discipline the viewer).[14]

In close second was a professor of English, Rob Wilson. His winning paragraph went like this:

If such a sublime cyborg would insinuate the future as post-Fordist subject, his palpably masochistic locations as ecstatic agent of the sublime superstate need to be decoded as the "now-all-but-unreadable DNA" of a fast deindustrializing Detroit, just as his Robocop-like strategy of carceral negotiation and street control remains the tirelessly American one of inflicting regeneration through violence upon the racially heteroglossic wilds and others of the inner city.[15]

Easy for him to say.

But it is not just academics who are speaking and acting in these interior codes reflecting a professional class or occupational elite. From the perspective of "outsiders" in this post-Christian culture, much of the church has been sounding tiny, tinny voices and views for decades.

✝ ✝ ✝

Thoughts are soaked in blood. The person meditating in his cave can influence the world as much as the person on the barricades.
—Philosopher Peter Marshall[16]

✝ ✝ ✝

KEEP OUT OF REACH OF CHILDREN

Morris County, Michigan (February 2000); Littleton, Colorado (April 1999); Paducah, Kentucky (December 1997); Ellis, Mississippi (October 1997); Jonesboro, Arkansas (March 1998); Edinborough, Pennsylvania (April 1998); Fayetteville, Tennessee (May 1998); Springfield, Oregon (May 1998) . . .

Lord knows, something needs to be done. Only the Lord isn't saying what that is.

Really? Might we already know what needs to be done and simply aren't doing it?

WIWAK (when I was a kid), we were taught to respect the power of "bad words." My parents' threat to "wash your mouth out with soap" was not a toothless bark. We learned the soapy way ("soap opera" had a very different connotation to me WIWAK) that certain words could soil our souls and foul our minds if we let them in.

> Sticks and stones can break my bones,
> but words can never hurt me.

Well, words do hurt. Words can do more than sting the body. "Bad words" can ravage and ruin the soul.

In the world in which we all now live, images have replaced words as the primary social currency. If "words" were capable of defiling one's life, "images" have umpteen times the power to contaminate and demoralize.

The mind is made up not of words, but of images. Doubt it? When you dream, what do you dream in: words or images? The earliest recorded languages of humans were picturegraphs. Images and metaphors come as close as human beings get to a universal language.

Metaphysics is metaphor. The molecules of our body are arranged by the metaphors of our mind. Images are the stuff of which the soul is sculpted. How did the Proverbs of Solomon phrase it? "As he thinketh in his heart, so is he" (Prov. 23:7 KJV). One of the greatest challenges of an EPIC church is to help its members create a healthy image-scape—not one controlled by popular culture but by every image that proceeds out of the mouth of God. Does the Holy Spirit moderate and monitor the meditations of your heart?

† † †

Postmoderns are virtually drowning.
—Erwin R. McManus[17]

† † †

We are the offspring of our outlook. Thoughts are literal "things." Especially when they take the form of images, thoughts are missiles you hurl from your head that can help or hurt others. Change your thoughts, and you change your life and the lives of those around you.

Parents are still teaching their children about "bad words" and refusing to allow their children to mouth certain words. But where is the prohibition against "bad images"? Where is the guidance in screening out of our children's eyes, as my parents soaped out of our mouths, "bad images"?

Kᴇᴇᴘ Oᴜᴛ ᴏꜰ Rᴇᴀᴄʜ ᴏꜰ Cʜɪʟᴅʀᴇᴍ

We brand this on all sorts of household products. Soap scrubbings can even brand this on words in our brains. Why don't we stamp this on certain images?

On an average day, a child will see two murders and thirty other acts of violence on television. We keep pornography under wraps and under the counter to "keep out of reach of children." Why don't we keep violent images under wraps and under the counters?

If we are the thoughts of our hearts, what are our hearts thinking? Cognitive theorists tell us that you and I generate at least sixty thousand thoughts a day. That amounts to one thought every 1.44 seconds. That thought may be true or false, noble or debased, just or unjust, pure or impure, lovable or spiteful, gracious or offensive, excellent or cheap, admirable or shameful. Since every thought reverberates biochemically throughout the body, our thoughts shape our souls in ways we have only begun to imagine. That is why the Scriptures say that whatsoever things are "true," "noble," "just," "pure," "lovable," "gracious," "excellent," and "admirable," "fill all your thoughts with these things" (Phil. 4:8 NEB).

Either we subjugate our thoughts to Christ or be subjugated by them. Part of the "whatsoever things" that must be brought under subjugation to Christ are not just visual: they are smells, tastes, touches, and sounds. Music theorist and critic Wilfrid Mellers doesn't listen to heavy metal because he says it is "propaganda for death."[18] Every sense has its own poison.

✝ ✝ ✝

It is not what you keep from a child that will save him, nor what town you move him to. It is what you put into him in the first place.
—*New York Times* editorial after Littleton[19]

✝ ✝ ✝

In one of the most memorable metaphors I have ever encountered, Robert Rabbin presents our predicament:

Imagine driving along Highway 5 in central California, going 75 miles an hour. Every 1.44 seconds your windshield cleaners spurt oil on your windshield. How can you see the road? How can you ever see what is actually there in front of you? This is what happens in us: a darkening and obscuring oil spurt goes off every 1.44 seconds. We cannot see through the oil spurts to where the real world is waiting. We act blindly and stupidly, at the mercy and effect of a process we aren't even aware of.[20]

What happens when we "fill our thoughts" and spray our windshield with violence and violation? In media culture, sex and violence seem to go together. Slasher movies are teens' favorite dating movies. Are they being told you can't have one without the other? Virtual violence, the kind we consume routinely on television, at the movies (Oliver Stone's *Natural Born Killers),* and in board and computer games *(Advanced Dungeons and Dragons, Duke Nukem, Grand Theft Auto, Magic: The Gathering),* doesn't sensitize us to killing and bloodshed. It desensitizes us. Screen violence conceives in us cravings for more killing and carnage. Digital killings don't actually cause us to be violent. But they create a conducive climate for original sin to bond with other risk factors.

The World Wildlife Fund discovered the paradoxical effect of violent images the hard way. Alarmed by the ruthless poaching of elephant tusks, in the late '80s the WWF decided to heighten the global awareness of the plight of these animals by showing pictures of how poachers obtain their tusks. In nothing flat, poachers tie the elephant down, take out a chain saw, slice off its face, rip away the ivory, and run off. Shortly after these horrid pictures appeared in magazines around the world, the WWF yanked them off the air.

Instead of sensitizing people to the plight of elephants, the WWF discovered to its horror that these violent images actually desensitized people to the crisis of the elephants and upped the ante of appetites for violent images.

Filmmaker Sam Peckinpah also discovered this the hard way. The increase in movie violence since the '60s was kindled by two masters of screen violence: Sam Peckinpah and Alfred Hitchcock. For Peckinpah violent images were a cultural critique of mindless and exploitative untraviolence. Under the guise of "catharsis," Peckinpah believed that heavy screen violence and savage images would challenge society's complacency about violence and work to reduce the incidence of violence in society. Peckinpah eventually repented of his ways when he saw that the movies he made like *The Wild Bunch* actually had the opposite effect. They "excited and energized audiences" to want to play out in real life the violence they saw on the screen.[21] Violent films promoted the same impulse that once made public executions so popular.

† † †

Tick, tick, tick, tick . . . Haa! That . . . shotgun is straight out of Doom.

—Murderer Eric Harris

† † †

The electronic game industry is a $16-billion business (twice the size of Hollywood's box-office gross). A child's primary learning method is based on rewards and punishments. What are we "learning" when violent games like

Postal (put out by a company named Running with Scissors) reward players for making multiple "kills" and punish players for not shooting to kill? What molecules are we making when we consume images of decapitations and play games where points are given for assassinating bystanders as well as bad guys? Still skeptical about how many kids are actually learning about life through computer games? Of kids six to twenty, 41 percent have game systems; 60 percent have computers; 99 percent have televisions in their homes. Eighty-seven percent of children aged eight to fourteen play video games, with an average time of 1.4 hours daily playing these video games. One of the Columbine shooters was addicted to ultraviolent video games. Here are two video game slogans for kids:

"Act locally, kill globally, unleash the beast within."
"You're serving up massive destruction, and roadkill is the main course."

The evidence linking GI to GO (garbage in, garbage out), violence in media to violence in society, is as compelling as the evidence connecting carbon dioxide to global warming, alcohol intake to fetal alcohol syndrome, or Lysol ingestion to intestinal poisoning. What we put into our minds is what we get out of our minds. So what are we putting into our minds? What are we putting into our souls?

What to do? Keep out of reach of children—violent and violating images. Teach them that just as there are "bad" words that one should never say, there are "bad" images that one should never see. And if one does see them (just as if one does say them), there needs to be a cleansing of the mind and body and repentance of the soul.

But parents can't do this alone. Hollywood is the image factory of the world. Hollywood (either willingly or unwillingly) must become an ally to families in their battle against a culture of bloodshed and violence addiction. The gaming industry's voluntary rating on all games and a public education campaign about what the ratings mean is not enough.

The French film director Jean-Jacques Annaud expressed the mission of his image-making in the following terms: "I want my images to carry an emotion you can hardly describe with words. They ring a secret bell in your heart, and those are the bells I love to ring."[22]

What if the bells in the heart a filmmaker loves to ring are not love and trust but hate, fear, brutality, horror? Kids themselves have for the first time ever rated violence, not drugs, as the biggest issue facing their generation today.[23]

No one wants censorship. No one wants to curb artistic bell-ringing. If your artistry as a filmmaker, videographer, or gamer requires heads to roll and bodies to be brutalized, go ahead and ring those bells. Feel free to create violent images just as you do now. But freedom entails responsibility. A license for anything costs.

So my proposal is this: To offset the social consequences of an image-maker's artistic freedom, a social tax of $10,000 per gratuitous violent image be levied to offset the social consequences of what Hollywood has created.

If you need one hundred acts of gratuitous violence to express yourself and create your movie/game/Web site, factor from the start a budget line of one million dollars that will go into a nonprofit foundation dedicated to youth-violence prevention and rehabilitation. In states like Florida, hotel guests pay a special levy to compensate the state for the environmental damages of laundry or dry-cleaning services. Let Hollywood image-makers pay a special levy on their production of "bad images" that can be used to rectify the messed up minds and maraudings of violence-saturated citizens and can compensate the country for the social, psychological, and economic costs of unfettered freedoms and violence consumption.

Of course, the ultimate solution to Florida's dry-cleaning pollution problem is a better way to clean suits.

The ultimate solution to postmodern culture's mental and moral pollution problem is a better way to clean hearts and fill them with the redeeming news of the gospel.

Fᴀɪᴛʜ Pʀᴀᴄᴛɪᴄᴇs ᴀɴᴅ Wᴇʙ Iɴᴛᴇʀᴀᴄᴛɪᴠᴇs

1. Discuss what one theologian may mean when the case is made that "metaphor is, for human beings, what instinctual groping is for the rest of the universe—the power of getting from here to there."[24]

2. Frederik Pohl is from Palatine, Illinois. In a letter-to-the editor column, he tells of a friend he calls "Joe." Joe is "a former CIA spook turned college professor who writes novels on the side."

> A while ago Joe began to write a novel about some near-future America in which terrorists went all out to cause as much damage as they could. He never finished writing it. By the time Joe got the first few chapters on paper, describing a few dozen ingenious but very practicable schemes for causing widespread misery and mayhem, his conscience began to bother him. He decided to destroy the manuscript, because he didn't want to give anybody ideas.

I never saw Joe's manuscript, and I don't know what particular schemes he had dreamed up. But they're not hard to invent. I've invented a few myself.

I know, for instance, how to destroy Boston Harbor, how to put the city of Chicago out of business for at least a week, and how to cut off traffic across any major bridge, using the services of no more than half a dozen men each—some can be done by a single individual—with the implements for doing these things easily available.

I don't intend to circulate any of these notions, because I don't want them on my conscience. But still, if I can think these things up, I'm sure that others can as well.

Discuss the restraint you find in this letter. Do you admire it? Is it necessary?

3. Listen to U2's *Pop* album, especially the songs like "Wake Up Dead Man," "If God Will Send an Angel," and "Playboy Mansion." To what extent would you call these songs "spiritual"?

4. It took very little time for Berliners to build an outside wall to keep people in. It will take many, many years for Berliners to take down the internal wall that will let them out, even though they are free as of 1989.

What is keeping your church from being let out into this new world brandishing images of Jesus the Christ that connect with the culture?

5. What are we to do about images of violence at the heart of Christianity? Isn't crucifixion a violent image? Is there a difference between the violence that comes from a culture of healing (surgery, martyrdom, heroism—laying down one's life for the sake of others, etc.) and the violence that comes from a culture of death (gunshots, gorging on gore, etc.). Is there a qualitative difference between salvific

violence versus sadistic violence? How can we tell the difference between the two?

6. Protestant Reformer Ulrich Zwingli articulated the
widespread Protestant belief that the money spent on the
images decorating the Catholic churches should be spent on
poor relief. For what were the poor if not the true images of
God? he asked. So the Protestants stripped churches of art-
work and divested books of "illuminations" or pictures.

What is wrong and right with this picture?

7. The church will need to create new ministries to deal
with the destructive powers of metaphors. For example, the
new kind of interactive hologram "entertainment" will no
doubt bring with it a whole new host of problems, mainly
addictions. These games can be played for decades, and some
players will literally become lost in the hologram, their iden-
tities submerged in their fantasies of favorite stars they are
playing out in their own private soap opera.

What other kinds of ministries can you anticipate for this
new world?

8. Charles Wesley taught Methodists to sing of the real
presence in their hymns.

9. Wes Nisker calls this the "crazy wisdom" of the truly
creative mind. Do you agree?

> Crazy wisdom sees that we live in a world of many illusions,
> that the Emperor has no clothes, and that much of human
> belief and behavior is ritualized nonsense. Crazy wisdom
> understands antimatter and old Sufi poetry; loves paradox
> and puns and pie fights and laughing at politicians. Crazy
> wisdom flips the world upside down and backward until
> everything becomes perfectly clear.[25]

10. Check out *www.lroom.org*. This church
(Lindenwood Christian Church, Memphis, Tennessee) offers

its members free Internet access. Is doing something similar a good idea for your church?

11. Postmoderns love mixed metaphors. Here's a new church called The Rock that has as its domain name "The Waters." Check out *www.thewater.org*. Sing the M. Gerald Derstine praise chorus "Jesus, Rock of Ages" (1973) that does the same. Its lyrics are:

> Jesus, Rock of Ages,
> let me hide myself in thee.
> Jesus, Living Water,
> let me drink from your flowing stream.

12. There is a well-known experiment in which baby finches were totally raised in a human environment for several generations. Then the researchers passed a silhouette of a paper hawk across their nest—and they shrieked in terror.

What images might be imprinted in the human soul?

13. "Every CEO wants to run a company that's totally focused on its customers. Every CEO wants to instill a can-do spirit, a sense that nothing is impossible. Every CEO wants to run a business that has not only the power of scale but also the soul of a startup. But bureaucracy gets in the way. The big-company way of doing things gets in the way."

Are these words of Martin Sorrell, chair and CEO of WPP Group PLC,[26] as relevant to the church as they are to the business world?

14. Is the world ruled more by people who say, "I have a dream" or, "I have a gun"?

15. For a portal to some of the best Christian Web sites, see *www.awesome-sites.com*.

16. Play the computer game *Myst*. Note how you are a central character. What other EPIC components can you identify?

Chapter Four

Epic Church for Epic Times

E-P-I-C(onnected)

eBay

Two favorite words used in the context of the Web are *connected* and *community*. In fact, the two words have become one in the new word *connexity*. Both eBay and Amazon.com say they are in the "connexity" business— making connections and building communities. Both demonstrate that the Web is less an information source than a social medium. Both are becoming the new town squares for the global village. At a time when many are lamenting the decline of "public space," the world is being wired to create a new kind of "public space": a global commons and a single marketplace.

The paradox is this: the pursuit of individualism has led us to this place of hunger for connectedness, for communities not of blood or nation but communities of choice. The very prevalence of the word *community* itself—is there any sector of society that isn't a "community"? (environmental community, gay community, Muslim community, Christian community)—betrays the absence of and craving for the real thing.[1]

After forty years of tracking USAmerican culture, sociologist Daniel Yankelovich concluded at the dawn of the twenty-first century: "My studies of the public reveal an immense pool of goodwill and good faith all over the country. Americans are hungry for enhanced quality of life, for deeper community, for endowing our communal life with spiritual significance."[2] Louise Conant, associate rector of Christ Church in Cambridge, Massachusetts, observes that whereas in the past "people came together in church on Sunday morning to celebrate the community that they had the rest of the week," people now "come to church on Sunday morning to find the community that they don't have the rest of the week."[3] Novelist Jan Karon's four-million-sold books testify to the hold on the postmodern imagination of USAmerica of small-town Mitfords that are spiritually rich and communally blessed.

The postmodern sense of community, however, is less nation-driven than culture-driven. The rise of private communities is one of the telltale signs of our times. Fifteen percent of USAmericans already belong to condominium, cooperative, or home-owner associations based on shared values and ruled by private governance.

A true Web site is a gathering place—a watering hole that people will go to so that they can meet other people who go there. Or in my case with eBay, a place where people who want to learn more about the material culture of Christianity, whale oil lamps, and classical dolphins can find one another, connect with one another, and start relationships.

More than buying and selling, the electronic emporium is about posting messages and Maydays on bulletin boards, policing the integrity of transactions through the Feedback Forum, discovering new friends, and launching new relationships at the eBay Café. The Internet is becoming a key relational tool both for kids—as 51 percent of teens use chat rooms to connect relationally with their peers—and for adults. Ask the question, "What are the most used resources on the Net?" and the answer is (1) information search engines, and (2) E-mail. Ask another question, "What accounts for the most time spent on the Net?" and the answer changes: chat rooms rank number one, consuming 26 percent of all time spent on the Internet.[4] One user said, "eBay and its cyber-incredible world is bringing people together to do a lot more than goods. We are trading our hearts."[5]

Don't laugh.

eBay may just be the closest experience of small-town USAmerica available to postmoderns. Where else can you harken back to that "nation of shopkeepers" where your word was your bond, your reputation was your credentials, your friendliness your trust, your voice your power? Where else can people tell the stories most central to who they are and find people eager to hear them? Where else can they participate so fully and have their lives changed by the experience?

Nowhere else.

Except, perhaps, the church. Our problem is this: the Web transforms the church's transactions both internally and with the outside world.

✝ ✝ ✝

To write a modern poem is to give voice not just to an "I," but to a "we," and the medium that makes that 'we' possible is what the poem represents as history. No agency . . . has been able to utter "we" so all-embracingly as Christianity, for it understands the sacred as the source of the secular and creates a "we," coextensive with "those for whom God died," which its own dynamic is continually forcing it to render more explicitly all-inclusive.

—Nicholas Boyle[6]

✝ ✝ ✝

FROM INDIVIDUAL TO INDIVIDUAL-COMMUNAL

Postmoderns have had it with religion. They're sick and tired of religion. They're convinced the world needs less of religion, not more. They want no part of obedience to sets of propositions and rules required by some "officialdom" somewhere. Postmoderns want participation in a deeply personal but at the same time communal experience of the divine and the transformation of life that issues from that identification with God. George Gallup, in his 1988 study of *The Unchurched American,* recommended as his number-one advice that the church stress religious experience over the institutional model of church by helping people experience God in their everyday lives.[7]

Why was Times Square the most popular place to greet the new millennium?

Why are coffee bars the new dating places?

Why is the Internet becoming less a disseminator of information and more a social medium?

Why are more and more people logging on, not to gain information but to hear, "You've got mail," and even to find love on-line?[8]

Why is the first thing a teen does after getting home from school is check E-mail and log on with friends?

Relationship issues stand at the heart of postmodern culture. As Apple Computer learned to its dismay, closed-system models are doomed to failure. Today it's all about relationships and partnerships. In classic and/also fashion, the more digitally enhanced the culture becomes, the more flesh-and-blood human the enchantments. The more impersonal the transactions (economic, social, etc.), the deeper the hunger for relationships and community. Remote-control experiences of recordings sharpen and strengthen rather than eat away at communal experiences of live performances.

Wild Ginger Philharmonic was founded in 1995 by David Goodman, a percussionist turned conductor. Weary of the way major orchestras treat their musicians "like puppets" and disgusted by performances that are more about technique than interpretation or soul, Wild Ginger Philharmonic is an orchestra which prizes individual creativity and exploration, a community where it is permissible to sound individual.

Why are musical students and members of prestigious orchestras willing to rehearse day and night for a week, then play a back-breaking concert tour in major cities along the east coast? Why are musicians willing to give up weeks of their time, not only for free but even funding their own participation?

In Wild Ginger, musicians can be part of a group while at the same time being personal. In Wild Ginger, interpretive judgments are made by consensus but are subject to being changed by moments of inspiration and individual spontaneity during the performances. Audiences don't just clap for Wild Ginger. They shout, jump, dance, and roar. Their enthusiasm is for an orchestral community where individual genius is celebrated and cultivated. As one observer puts it, "There's a germ of a new paradigm here, a new approach to classical musicianship"[9] in which the individual and communal are fused together.

WORD-OF-MOUSE COMMUNITIES

Few have even begun to think through the social and ecclesial ramifications of living in a digital culture. By 1998, the digital economy was growing at double the rate of the overall economy. The biggest manufacturing in USAmerica is not automobiles, it now turns out, but information technology. One-third of the total USAmerica economy is already being "reassigned" because of the Internet, one expert calculates, even forcing one mall to try to prohibit its retail tenants from promoting any and all purchasing of merchandise over the Internet.[10] It's a futile ban. The U.S. Department of Commerce says that Internet use is doubling every one hundred days and that electronic commerce should reach $300 billion by 2002.[11] Twenty-five percent of the USAmerican workforce will be headquartering out of homes in the next five years, another sociologist insists.[12]

The Internet is proving to be one of the greatest inventions in the history of civilization. The primary arenas of social exchange and community engagement—workplace, shopping malls, supermarkets—are being marginalized in a culture where sources of community are already hard to come by.[13] The more connected we become electronically, the more disconnected we can become personally. One psychiatrist has a patient who calls her husband's computer "his plastic mistress."[14]

The new cyberfriends and connections one finds in e-life will only stir up the hunger for face-to-face community. The more wired to the world our electronic cottages (castles?) become, the more the church will need to be a place that can form authentic community where individuals can be free to be themselves. The words St. Augustine addressed to God ring anew in postmodern ears: "Where I am most inwardly myself, there You were far more than I."

The heart of postmodernity is a theological dyslexia: me/we, or the experience of individual-in-community. It is less the case that, as William Tyndale first noticed, the word *myself* does not appear in the Gospels. It is more that in the Gospels no individual "I" can become "myself" without "you" and "others." Postmoderns want to enjoy a self-identity within a connectional framework of neighborliness, civic virtue, and spiritual values.

That is why the C in EPIC stands for "connectedness" rather than for "community." The negative connotations to "community" only begin with words like *bigotry, narrowness, nosiness, conformism.* Just read Sherwood Anderson, Theodore Dreiser, Willa Cather, William Faulkner, to name only a few modern novelists.

But even people who are shy, socially challenged, or who find "community" painful and persecuting need connectedness—a connectedness that can come partly from nature, from beauty, from ritual, from family, from animals, but a connectedness that comes most wholly and holy only from God.

† † †

To get singled out is to get picked off.
—Robert G. Tuttle, Jr.

† † †

The church exists to incarnate connectedness and to inculcate greater consciousness of connectedness. At any moment, however ordinary and uneventful, "me" is inextricably connected to "we." Even when I am most alone, "I" am connected to and dependent on a global mix of "us" cultures and languages totally foreign to my first-person self.

> I sit at my word processor (assembled here in the USA with chips made in Japan) in a pair of Levis sewn in Mexico while wearing a British brand of sneakers (Reeboks) which, a discreet tag inside informs, was manufactured in South Korea. For lunch, I will eat a salad made from vegetables grown in South Florida which were harvested by a vast army of migrant workers who are Hispanic or contract workers from the Caribbean.[15]

Be=We/Me

Think back on the flowers that were strewn on the side-walks as part of Princess Diana's funeral. Something registered in your subconscious about those mounds of flowers, even if you didn't call it to rational or verbal consciousness. Can you pull it out? What was unique about those flowers?

In the medieval world, where everything was communal and nothing was individual, grieving villagers were content simply to pile flowers on top of other flowers. In the modern world, where everything was individual and little was communal, single bouquets of flowers were arranged in individual vases and put on the altar or grave. In postmodern culture we put our flowers back on the communal pile but attach individual notes to the flowers and wrap them in cellophane or plastic to separate them from the crowd.

A postmodern "me" needs "we" to "be." In the modern world, it was "I think, therefore I am." The postmodern sensibility loops back to the premodern before it becomes post-modern. Among the Xhosa people of southern Africa, it has always been: "I am because we are."[16]

Electronic culture necessitates longer pastoral tenures, not shorter. Building relationships of trust and intimacy in a pre-Christian culture takes time. The transiency of the culture requires that our community building and hospitality be more aggressive, not less; more premeditated, not haphazard. Dietrich Bonhoeffer's conviction that an anti-Christian culture can actually work for the good of Christianity presupposes a vibrant, connected life (whether above or underground, prosaic or heroic) where people of faith can teach one another to live by faith—which is what God intended in the first place.

✝ ✝ ✝

> *Let him alone, let him*
> *have his way, let him be touched*
> *by his own angel, it will come to nothing:*
> *born again, but stillborn.*
> —Contemporary British poet Geoffrey Hill[17]

✝ ✝ ✝

The future promises a rapture of communal customs and values. Postmoderns are disillusioned with the hyperindividualism of high modernity. In the words of Gen-Xer Tom Beaudoin, "My generation inherited not free love but AIDS, not peace but nuclear anxiety, not cheap communal lifestyles but crushing costs of living, not free teach-ins but colleges priced for aristocracy."[18] Part of this quest for community and connected dimensions of life appear retro and neotraditional: white wedding gowns, dance halls (swing dancing, ballroom dancing), even church fellowship halls.

But the individual quest for communal rituals is deep. To address this hunger for community, an EPIC church will need to upgrade four avenues of ministry.

PUT THE SALVE IN SALVATION

Connectedness, the first avenue of ministry to be upgraded, is the key to physical and emotional health. If you feel "connected," you will live longer, live healthier, live happier.[19] The famous Alameda County Study conducted by Professor Lis Berkman discovered that patients who were least connected were three times more likely to die in that nine-year period under study than those who had stronger social ties.[20]

The church needs to reinvent the concept of "connection" and "connectedness" to fit a postmodern context. It is not just the extensiveness of connection that counts but the diversity of connections that make a difference. Postmoderns also need to learn the difference between a life rich in connections and a life rich in contacts or rich in networking.[21] One Harvard psychiatrist has isolated twelve connections we need to make in life if we are to be "well connected": our family of origin, our immediate family, our friends and community, our work world, the world of art and beauty, a connection with our heritage, with nature, with pets, with ideas and information, with social groups, with ourselves. But the greatest connection of all we need to establish is our connection with God.[22]

God is the Ultimate Connection: "I will never leave you or forsake you" (Heb. 13:5 NRSV). Some of the most healing words of Scripture are God's promises of connectedness: "I will be with you," and, "I am with you always, even to the end of the age" (cf. Exod. 3:8–12; Matt. 28:20). The power of connection is a healing power. Healing connections are here, there, and everywhere for the picking if the church can help postmoderns understand what it means to be connected—connected to one another, connected to creation, even connected to the church itself.

Three-quarters of all pastors see themselves as gifted at either teaching or preaching.[23] Yet Jesus' ministry had three components: preaching, teaching, and healing. If moral and spiritual transformation is to occur communally as well as individually, pastors will need to upgrade their healing role and hone their healing skills to at least the same levels as preaching and teaching.

All three components of ministry must have delivery systems on-line. The church can't "create" community on-line, but it can cultivate it and water it and grow it into preaching, teaching, and healing digital stations of the cross. The Internet enables one little church in Iowa or Iceland to preach, teach, and heal millions (soon billions) of people.

The only thing standing in our way is a lack of creativity.

The Complex Art of Simple Living

The second upgraded avenue of ministry concerns, like everything else in postmodern culture, the need for the church to be decentralized and complexified.[24]

Complexity is good. Look at how God created the universe: self-healing rhino horns; rats able to chew through metal; nuclear fallout-surviving beetles; spider silk stronger than steel and tougher than kevlar (parachutes).[25] How is this possible?

Because of complexity of design. Abalone shell is 98 percent chalk. Yet it has a breaking strength that is twice that of any high-tech ceramic composite. Why? Its flat, hexagonal chalk particles are stacked on top of one another between layers of organic matter that act as flexible mortar, increasing its strength factor by twenty times and making it behave like a metal.

Strength and power come through complexity, not simplicity—the complexity of a network, not the simplicity of a line.

Postmodern culture brings in its wake a double edge toward global hypercentralization and local decentralization. Examples of local decentralization at work are all around us:

- The one big refrigerator has been replaced by refrigerators you can find in places other than kitchens—bedrooms, family room bars, playrooms, grill areas, custom-installed in any cabinet or drawer.
- Already the California state legislature has considered two proposals to divide California into two new states.
- Already some twenty-five counties have voted to secede from California.

What would it mean to decentralize something like worship? Worship must become a key component to every small, separate cell group that is free to worship in its own way while integrated into the larger church. Eighty-five percent of churches now offer cell-group opportunities, each one of which should include a worship component. At the same time, hypercentralized worship services, where the whole body comes together for celebrations, become more important than ever.

† † †

Not to be encompassed by the greatest, but to let oneself be encompassed by the smallest—that is divine.
—Epitaph for St. Ignatius of Loyola[26]

† † †

At the same time of local decentralization, there is global hypercentralization. The world is adjusting to a new global economy and a new global society. Postmodern churches need to be born global. When you plant a church, begin with the awareness that your potential congregation is five billion "members."

The web of connections that bind us all together is only beginning to be appreciated by the church. We rise or fall together. Does it matter that Africa is being ravaged right now by AIDS, that Russia is being ravaged right now by unemployment, that Turkey is being ravaged right now by earthquakes, that California is being ravaged right now by fires, that Jupiter is being bombarded right now by asteroids?

You bet it does. Their future is our future. We are so interconnected that what happens either next door or next planet triggers responses throughout the universe.

Next door. Historically, and especially during the nineteenth century, fire became a major concern for the world's rapidly growing cities. Closely built wooden buildings, replete with open-hearth fireplaces, gas lamps, flaming candles, and billowing draperies created a highly combustible atmosphere that often led to massive fires with huge losses of life and property.

Private fire-fighting companies quickly arose in response to this desperate human need. In exchange for monthly or annual fees, these companies promised property owners that they would come and put out any fires on their property.

> Ah, but such an arrangement had a fatal flaw. If your next door neighbor had neglected to purchase fire fighting protection or could not afford to purchase it, his fire went unquenched, and swiftly became a raging inferno that engulfed your property.
>
> So in the cities people then turned to the public sector for a solution, as they often do when confronted with one of these "we-are-all-in-the-same-boat-together" situations. And the modern-day public fire department, which we now all take for granted, was born.[27]

Next planet. An asteroid hit the planet Jupiter not long ago. The Shoemaker-Levy comet broke apart and hit Jupiter's atmosphere with the force of several million thermonuclear bombs.

What does this have to do with a discussion of community? Everything. Without the gravitational muscle of planet Jupiter, Earth could not be the garden planet of the Milky Way galaxy. Jupiter is a celestial Venus fly trap that yanks away from Earth's gravitational field killer asteroids and meteroids, taking into her bosom the explosions that would rip Earth apart.[28] Every now and then a couple of smaller rocks get by Jupiter's snapping tongue, but the more juicy ones that would destroy Earth have already been gobbled up.

† † †

Story molds us. There's hardly anything we change our minds about because we're convinced of it by logical arguments. Story makes us who we are.
                    —Robyn Miller, creator of
                    the classics *Myst* and *Riven*[29]

† † †

WELL-STORIED

Storytelling, the third upgraded avenue of ministry, creates community. The narrative quality of experience is a deeply religious issue. We organize our experience through narrative. We inhabit a storied reality.[30] Human cognition is based on storytelling. Or as one researcher puts it, stories are "the fundamental instrument of thought."[31]

The modern world privileged abstract principles over "stories." In fact, the poet John Betjeman defined an intellectual as simply a nonvisual person.[32] The very word *abstract* comes from the Greek *ab*, which means "to move away from," and *strahere,* which means "to stand." To have an abstract relationship with something, one has to stand away from it. To tell a story, one has to step into it and hold it tightly. In fact, according to New Testament scholar Tom Boomershine, "To say 'Let me tell you a story' is like saying, 'Let's go play.'"33

> The gospel has lost its original character as a living story-telling tradition of messengers who told the good news of the victory of Jesus. . . . Telling biblical stories is foreign to contemporary experience. We continue to read Bible stories to children. But the assumption is that once you grow up and learn to think you will stop telling stories and start telling the truth. Telling the truth means you will speak in conceptual abstractions.34

The language of the Scriptures is story. You can tell stories and never use words, much less words that come to a point. In fact, the story of the Gospels is told most effectively with bread and wine—images and elements of the earth, images and elements you can taste, touch, see, smell, and hear. Postmoderns need to be able to taste, touch, hear, smell, and see this story of Jesus.

Telling stories in a digital culture may take any number of learning and worship forms—oral, audio, video, TV, films, multimedia, CD-rom, print, as well as the place where all the above converge into one: www.

Get Moving

Enactive worship that leads to service and social transformation is the fourth upgraded avenue of ministry. In the words of religious studies scholar Huston Smith, "The heart of religion is not altered states but altered traits of character.

For me, then, the test of a substance's religious worth or validity is not what kind of far-out experience it can produce, but is the life improved by its use?"[35]

Once upon an eternity, St. Peter greeted three new arrivals at the Pearly Gates. He began their heavenly orientation with a question: "What would you like most to hear your family and friends say about you at your funerals?"

The first replied, "I would be most gratified to hear them say that I lived a useful life as a doctor and as a family man."

The second replied, "I would be happy to hear them say that I was an excellent school teacher, a wonderful wife and mother, and an asset to my community."

Said the third, "I would like to hear them say, 'Look! He's moving!'"

The history of Christianity could be written in two volumes of about equal size. One would feature the story of those who, when they got the message, hung up, got moving, and turned their lives "to do good works" (Eph.2:10 NIV).

The other would feature the story of those who never hung up.[36]

For ecstaticants to become actants, forget an annual mission Sunday. Make every day a mission day and every worship service a mission service. In fact, worship services need the double vision of what they say they are: worship service.

† † †

*Holy ground is never private turf
but always communal space.*
—Kenda Creasy Dean and Ron Foster[37]

† † †

Not Silver, Not Gold, Not Even Platinum

All I wanted was a soft pretzel sans butter. "Sorry, sir, we don't serve pretzels without butter," the attendant announced as she removed from the oven steaming, hot pretzels which she proceeded to dip into the butter.

"You don't understand," I explained hurriedly, as my plane was boarding its final passengers from Newark's Continental C Terminal. "Just hand me the pretzel from the oven. Don't dip it into the butter. I'll pay you full price for it."

"Sorry, sir, we don't serve pretzels without butter."

I had no time to argue, and I was hungry. "I've had no-butter pretzels at better establishments than this all over the country. But let's not argue. This is what I'll do. Here's a $5 bill. That's almost three for one. You keep the change. Just hand me that one pretzel there without butter. Deal?"

"No, sir. We don't serve pretzels without butter."

"Can you tell me why?"

"I can't imagine a soft pretzel without butter. I certainly wouldn't serve you one."

"Let me get this right," I asked in total amazement. "You are refusing to sell me one pretzel when I'm willing to pay the price of three of them because I want you to leave off the butter?"

"That's right sir. We don't serve pretzels without butter."

I walked on the plane with no pretzel but with a great illustration of Golden Rule religion at work. Golden Rule Christianity is squelching our communities, our churches, our businesses, our faith. The Golden Rule kept me from getting a pretzel.

The Golden Rule is based on putting who first? "Do unto others as *you* would have them do unto you." The attendant refused to serve me a pretzel because she couldn't conceive of a pretzel without butter. She was doing unto me as *she* would have done unto her.

Jesus broke the Golden Rule and broached a new rule. He called it "the New Commandment" (John 13). I call it the Titanium Rule.

> "I give you a new commandment: love one another; as I have loved you, so you are to love one another. If there is this love among you, then all will know that you are my disciples" (John 13:34–35 NEB)

We are to do unto others . . . how? Not as *we* would have others do to us. Not even as *others* would have us do unto them. The business revolution of the '70s and '80s was precisely this move away from me-centered to others-centered, customer-driven service. Companies no longer sell what they produce, they produce what others want to buy. Tony Alessandra calls this "The Platinum Rule."[8] Do unto others as others would have you do unto them.

Why Jesus Prefers Titanium

Jesus' Titanium Rule took it one step farther from the Platinum Rule, two steps farther than the Golden Rule, three steps farther than the Silver Rule (love those who love you: eye for eye/tooth for tooth), and four steps farther than the Iron Rule (do unto others before they do it unto you). We are to do unto others as Jesus has done unto us. And how has Jesus treated us?

✝ ✝ ✝

*This is my commandment: love one another, as I have
loved you. There is no greater love than this, that a man
should lay down his life for his friends. You are my
friends, if you do what I command you.*
                                    —Jesus (John 15:12–14 NEB)

✝ ✝ ✝

Jesus loved us so much that he was willing to "lay down"
some things for us. He laid down his eighteen-year career; he
laid down his security; he laid down his reputation; he laid
down his relatives; he even laid down his life for us. The
Titanium Rule asks this question: What are you willing to
"lay down" for others that they might pick up life and health
and truth?

Two of the hottest authors on the investment circuit
today are the Motley Fool Gardner brothers, David and
Tom. Their blockbuster book *Rule Breakers, Rule Makers*
(1999) is breaking all the rules and making some new ones.[39]

Their call for leaders to become "rule breakers, rule
makers" is echoed by two consultants from the Gallup
organization. They surveyed more than eighty thousand
managers in four hundred companies and authored a book
about their findings: *First, Break All the Rules: What the
World's Greatest Managers Do Differently* (1999).[40]

- Fred Smith broke the rule that only the U.S. Post
  Office could deliver mail: and founded Federal
  Express.
- Steve Jobs broke the rule that computers couldn't be
  designed for home use: and founded Apple Computer.

- Lunsford Richardson broke the rule that all mail had to go to a name. He convinced the U.S. Post Office to let him send mail to "Boxholder" (now "Occupant"), thereby jump-starting Vick's VapoRub.

- Anita Roddick broke the rule that said cosmetics were only about glamour and fantasy. She said they were about health and well-being. Instead of high-priced packaging, the company she founded used plastic refillable bottles. You can find this cosmetics company called The Body Shop in almost every mall and most major airport concourses.

- Leo Burnett broke the rules that said words were advertising. He said images were: and gave us Tony the Tiger, the Jolly Green Giant, the Marlboro Man, the Pillsbury Doughboy, the Keebler elves, Morris the Cat, etc.

- Howard Schultz broke the rules about coffee. In 1987, the big three (General Foods, Procter & Gamble, and Nestle) had locked up nearly 90 percent of the USAmerican coffee market. They thought they were invincible. While they conducted business as usual, Starbucks capitalized on the fact that customer priorities were changing from price to quality and cashed in. Within five years Starbucks and similar roasters jointly owned 22 percent of the national coffee market, about one billion dollars.

The original Rule Breaker, Rule Maker? Jesus of Nazareth. Jesus' personal presence suspends all the rules, overturns all the conventions, and inaugurates the rules of a new kingdom—a new heaven and a new earth.

- Jesus broke the rules of religion: he healed on the Sabbath, ate unclean food, didn't fast when he was supposed to.
- Jesus broke the rules of philosophy: at a time when truth was found in tradition and custom, Jesus found truth in relationships and people.
- Jesus broke the rules of economics: when perfume was squandered lavishly, Jesus rebuked those who didn't understand the imperative of beauty and presence.
- Jesus broke the rules of society: he ate with untouchables, talked to women, touched lepers, welcomed children into the kingdom, privileged the poor, and generally crossed every social boundary of his day.
- Jesus broke the rules of propriety: accused of eating and drinking too much, Jesus chided his critics: "We piped to you, and you didn't dance."
- Jesus even broke the ultimate rule: the law of sin and death. He broke our captivity to "principalities and powers." He broke the ruling powers of the grave and made rebirth possible for all.

Jesus the Rule Breaker violated the house rules and left us with one big Titanium Rule: "Love one another."

Jesus the Rule Maker gave us the rule that trumps all other rules: "Love one another as I have loved you." It is the Titanium Rule—named after the hardest metal and the hardest rule to keep—that is to characterize our lives of connectedness. In Jesus' phrasings, we are to "lay down" or bury" our own self-interests and "take up the Cross" (Matthew 16) so that others may pick up the truth.

† † †

*For which is greater, the gift or the altar that makes
the gift sacred.*

—Matthew 23:19 NRSV,
on the importance
of sacred communities

† † †

İ'ᴅ Rᴀᴛʜᴇʀ Hᴀᴠᴇ Jᴇsᴜs Tʜᴀⴖ Sɪʟᴠᴇʀ ᴏʀ Gᴏʟᴅ

Jesus is the Truth. Truth resides in relationships, not documents or principles. The Gospels don't teach us about Jesus
as principle but Jesus as person. The power of a logo is that
it transmutes image into identity, creating the very thing it
symbolizes. In Jesus, the logos and logo became one.

Not until the fourteenth century (at the earliest) did truth
become embedded in propositions and positions.[41] The shift
from "troth" to "truth" was the shift from truth residing in
relationships to truth being found in documents and evidence. The spread of a literate print culture and changes in
governmental authority meant that by the Renaissance this
new scientific sense of truth as something independently ver-
ifiable was well established. But truth as doctrine, truth as a
system of belief, truth as propositions that exist apart from
those who incarnate truth spelled a profound social and religious change in the history of Western culture.

When "truth" could not be understood apart from the
network of relationships connecting people to one another;

when "truth" had no independent status outside of obligations to God and to others: the biblical admonitions of

"I am the way, and the truth, and the life" (John 14:6
NRSV)

"You will know the truth, and the truth will make you
free" (John 8:32 NRSV)

"When the Spirit of truth comes, he will guide you into
all the truth" (John 16:13 NRSV)

had a very different ring to them. The quaint "plight thee my
troth" language beckons us back to a biblical drama where
Truth was embodied in a person, where Truth resided in a
relationship with the very image and incarnation of God.

Someday I will hold up my Bible before a congregation,
shake it, and yell at the top of my lungs, "This is not a book
primarily about propositions and programs and principles.
This is a book about relationships. This is a primer in connectedness. This is a book about you and God's love for you
in God's only begotten Son." Or in the words of Hugh Ross
Mackintosh: "When once the Gospel has been severed from
a historic person, and identified with a complex of meta-
physical ideas, what it ought to be called is scarcely worth
discussion; that it is no longer Christianity, is clear."[42]

Jesus himself is the Truth.

Jesus himself is the Kingdom.

Jesus himself is the Life.

Before God and all witnesses, I plight my "troth" to Jesus
the Christ.

Faith Practices and Web Interactives

1. Check out "Z-Games" on the Disney Channel. Kids E-mail in their favorite made-up games. Then the producers send a camera crew out to video the kids doing the game. They even use the "kid-cam" to get a POV shot of the kids playing. In another segment the kids are given a variety of objects and must make up a game in twenty minutes.

2. Discuss this statement: "People who think and write about church growth perhaps should pay a little more attention to the Book of Acts. The earliest Christians simply acted like Christians, like friends and followers of Jesus. They devoted themselves to love and compassion. It doesn't say they devoted themselves to church growth or evangelism. It says they devoted themselves to caring for one another and for others, and the world was compelled by their authenticity, the integrity of the life they lived in the world. Their life together was the very best evangelism."[43]

3. It is estimated that 20 percent of the production of all domestic companies takes place outside of USAmerica. Here is a shipping label on a USAmerican electronics producer: "Made in one or more of the following countries: Korea, Hong Kong, Malaysia, Singapore, Taiwan, Mauritius, Thailand, Indonesia, the Philippines. The exact country of origin is unknown."

Companies who receive two-thirds or more of their revenue abroad include Exxon, Colgate-Palmolive, Manpower, Mobil, Coca-Cola. Companies with 50 percent or more of revenue from foreign sales: Avon, Gillette, IBM, Citicorp, Xerox, McDonald's, Dow, Intel, Hewlett-Packard, Texas Instruments, Kodak, 3K, Texaco, Ralston Purina, and P&G.

To what extent is the "connected" component of EPIC a global community? How can the church rid itself of its globalphobia?

4. There are more than five hundred thousand houses of worship in USAmerica. What are these spaces doing to make their community and world better? In spite of our tax exemption, how many of our churches sit empty most of the time?

5. Faith-based community economic development (CDC) has been defined as

> a process through which residents and other community stakeholders engage in social, economic, housing and other asset development. The goal is to build and sustain healthy communities through the creation of jobs and business enterprises; the production of decent affordable housing, and the forging of enduring institutions—both physical and social— which educate and support families and individuals. Faith-based community development engages in this process as the expression of religious or spiritual ministry, calling or beliefs.[44]

In 1995, South Tampa Christian Center (STCC) created a community development corporation called REACT (Restoration and Evangelism Advanced Through Community Training). REACT umbrellas four ministries: a medical clinic called Synergy; a vocational-technical school; a GED program; and an accredited school for at-risk children called Life Skills Learning Center. Research the CDCs in your area.

6. It is the Holy Spirit who energizes us, enabling us to come to saving faith in Jesus Christ, to grow in our knowledge of him. The Holy Spirit is the same one who then

deploys us in servant ministries to others. John A. Juffman Jr. writes:

> Lloyd Ogilvie tells how he tried to illustrate to his congregation decades ago in Bethlehem, Pennsylvania, how important it was that we realize we have a two-legged gospel. It's so easy to emphasize either personal faith or social responsibility. He tried to clarify that to walk or run with the Master takes both *personal faith* and *social responsibility*. So what he did was preach the first five minutes of his sermon standing on his right leg.
>
> He preached hard about faith. Because it was an enclosed pulpit, the people did not see that he was on one leg. As he neared the end of the first five minutes, his balance on one leg was lost, and he fell toward the left, catching himself with a quick grasp on the pulpit side. Then the same was repeated on the left leg. As he preached about social responsibility, he continued until he, once again, lost his balance.
>
> Then he spent the rest of the sermon explaining why we must stand, walk, and run with Christ on both legs of the gospel. He then made the disclaimer that if he'd done something like that every Sunday in the years as pastor, he would have been accused of showmanship.
>
> Yet he notes that anytime he returns to Bethlehem, Pennsylvania, someone reminds him of that sermon. Years of rhetoric about wholesome discipleship got focused in a carefully selected, physical movement. Never forget, God is interested in complete healing.
>
> Ours is a spiritual and a social gospel. It is a call to repentance and faith in Jesus Christ combined with a willingness to go out into the community with a cup of cold water in his name.[45]

7. Here is a note General George Washington wrote to the

Members of the Volunteer Association and Other Inhabitants of the Kingdom of Ireland Who Have Lately Arrived in the City of New York, 2 December 1783: The bosom of America is open to receive not only the Opulent and respectable Stranger, but the oppressed and persecuted of all Nations and Religions whom we shall welcome to a participation of all our rights and privileges, if by decency and propriety of conduct they appear to merit the enjoyement.[46]

Is George Washington right in his assessment of USAmerica?

8. J. Leslie Houlden, in a review of *The Cambridge Companion to Biblical Interpretation*, ed. John Barton (Cambridge: Cambridge University Press, 1999), ends with this comment that needs the church's attention and discussion:

Finally, . . . only two writers (Robert Morgan and John Barton) pay any notable attention to the relation between modern biblical studies and the Bible's main home: the Christian Churches. That's the measure of the Enlightenment's force, and of a situation that seems to be of little serious concern to most in either party.[47]

9. For the Lord's Prayer in 770 languages and dialects, see *http://www.christusrex.org/www1/pater/index.html*.

10. Listen to the song "Bullet with Butterfly Wings" in Smashing Pumpkins' *Mellon Collie and the Infinite Sadness*. Discuss Billie Corgan's longing for a relationship with God like Jesus had as reflected in these lyrics:

tell me I'm the only one
tell me there's no other one
Jesus was an only son
tell me I'm the chosen one
Jesus was an only son for you

11. For global experiences of community, check out *www.well.com* or *www.garden-web.com*, especially the

Garden Party sector. I dare you: ask a garden question that can't be answered by one of the fifteen thousand users from around the world who check into this site on a daily basis. Or check out *tabletalk.salon.com*, perhaps the most sophisticated popular discussion forum on-line.

12. Explore the eBay Website. Bid on something. Follow the transaction from beginning to end. Do you agree that

> the emerging auction economy is about rules, honor, trust and integrity as much as it is about buying and selling. And it's about individual consumers, not the marketplace, assigning value to products. Like so many other trends, it's further proof that the individual is becoming the single most important economic unit, and that community still matters.[48]

13. For theologian Dietrich Bonhoeffer, community is simply our life in Christ. "No Christian community is more or less than this. Whether it be a brief, single encounter or the daily fellowship of years, Christian community is only this. We belong to one another only through and in Jesus Christ."[49] Where does and doesn't this statement resonate with your spirit?

14. What do you think about the GardenWeb's one-time rule for on-line discussion: "No religion, no politics."

15. For a feeling of community online, check out *www.churchwerx.com*.

16. WAREHOUSE, an offshoot of a Billy Graham mission to England, is an EPIC church being held at St. Cuthbert's Church, Peasholme Green, York. Services are at 8 P.M. on the first (celebration service) and third (communion) Sundays of the month.

There is ambient dance music; people sit in rings around a central table covered in candles and bread and wine. Art is everywhere. There are TV monitors everywhere and slide projectors which place religious art on the walls.

They are focused on people in the club scene.

See *http://www.abbess.demon* . . . paradox/docs.

17. Ignatius Loyola in his *The Spiritual Exercises* recommended that you become a character in a biblical story until you literally "feel it." Imagine yourself in the story until you can touch, taste, see, hear, and smell the scenes and characters.

18. In 1970, when the black scholar Angela Davis was placed on the FBI's ten most wanted list, the number of USAmericans in prison stood at 196,429. It has since soared to more than two million. What does this say (if anything) about the quality of our communities?

† † †

Endtroduction

Theoretical Backgrounding

On the night he proposed to the girl of his dreams, a young man decided it was time to tell all. "Before you say yes, my love," he said, "there is something I must tell you—something that might change your feelings toward me. You see, I am a somnambulist."

The young lady thought for a moment, then replied, "Oh, that's all right. There's no problem. I'm a Methodist. We can go to your church one Sunday and to mine the next."

For a church that is worshiping at the Chapel of the Somnambulists, Jesus issues these words of warning: "Stay awake." "And what I say to you," Jesus urged, "I say to all: Keep awake" (Mark 13:37 NRSV). Or on another occasion Jesus instructs his sleepwalking disciples to live wisely and "stay awake, because you do not know either the day or the hour" (Matt. 25:13 NJB).

This chapter is written for those who wish to "wake up" not just to the bracing winds of this postmodern world but to the secular influences and sources that are shaping postmodern thought and culture. This "endtroduction" is not for those faint of heart and gizzard. One must have both a high tolerance for theorrhoea (academic theorizing) and a low threshold for transparency. But for those wanting a closer reading of the theories and theses that are in intellectual currency these days, this chapter is designed to help you cut a path in the wilderness.

A DIVIDED CHRISTENDOM

Christendom is divided today between Old World Churches and New World Churches.

They move at different speeds.

They prize different values.

They measure success differently.

They think differently: one primarily in terms of big and small; the other in terms of fast and slow.

One is book-centric, the other Web-centric. In one, the book is the foundation of everything they do. In the other, the Web is their defining metaphor and mechanism.

You can't avoid the stench of ecclesiastical disintegration or the sweet aroma of new growth.

✝ ✝ ✝

We live in a world that is half dead and half born.
—Billy O. Wireman, President, Queens College

✝ ✝ ✝

Old World Churches
"Write it Down"

The Old World Church refuses to change its culture to become more accessible. It either refuses to believe that anything much has changed in the culture or wants to live a separated lifestyle. Those few Old World Churches who understand that it is a new world out there approach the culture with the following spirit: "Stop the world, the church wants to get on."

But the world refuses to stop. And there is no hiding place. Old World Churches profoundly misunderstand the world we live in. More than puzzled by and nervous about the virtualization of the church, they are virtually paralyzed by thoughts about what it means to become an E-P-I-C church. They do not use the Internet other than as brochureware.

New World Churches
"As for Me and My Mouse"

New realities are fundamentally changing the way these churches operate. The New World Church constitutes a new ecclesiastical ecosystem that has changed not just how the church functions, but also what it means to be the body of Christ.

The New World Church wants to live not a separated lifestyle from the world, but a sanctified lifestyle in the world. It is reverent about the message and agnostic about the medium. Its models of success have shifted from bigness to speed, which can become as idolic as bigness was to the Old World Church. The New World Church centralizes complexity and decentralizes simplicity.

The New World Church understands that the Age of Print is over. Print is not the only privileged style of communication. Truth resides in doings as much as documents. New World Churches use the Web to deliver new ministries, improve the core ministries that already exist, and heighten relationships among members. Members of the New World Church don't live on the browser. But . . .

"As for me and my mouse, we will serve the Lord."

E-P-I-C METHODOLOGY

One of the biggest differences between Old World Churches and New World Churches is the embrace of E-P-I-C methodologies. The Old World Church is trapped in monocular outlooks where the divine is "out there" to be hauled "in here" by objective methods.

The postmodern pilgrim does not seek new truths, but seeks with new eyes eternal truths. The postmodern pilgrim sees with both eyes a world that exists and extends beyond ourselves while at the same time is a creation of ourselves.

The three schools of thought and culture helping to create this E-P-I-C methodology are as follows:

- Postmodern hermeneutics
- Hard sciences
- Cognition research

Hermeneutics is the science of interpretation, especially of the Bible. Christendom's predominant model of performance-based church cannot hold up under postmodern hermeneutics and philosophy. It is helpful to remember that just as the Protestant Reformation was a worship revolution wrought by changes in hermeneutics and epistemology, so the current Postmodern Reformation is witnessing revolutions in worship styles and functions wrought by similar intellectual forces.

POSTMODERN HERMENEUTICS

Why has praise music been such a pet hate in so many church circles? Even when a pop figure like Barbara Streisand comes forward and announces her favorite praise song ("Holy Ground"), the church's railings against "praise choruses" as one of the vices of the age remain shrill. Why such modernist posings against "praise"?

The scientific method was a "critical" method. Moderns were trained to critique not to cheerlead, to exegete not to extol, to assess not to applaud, to take apart not to put together. The paradox of the phrase "this is critical" being itself positive was lost on a culture that climbed to the highest observation points for investigating anything, including the divine.

The postmodern hermeneutics of participant-observation, first pioneered by the Polish-born British anthropologist Bronislaw Malinowski, are dethroning the old epistemological pretensions of knowing predicated on the posturings of arm's-length analysis and under-glass understandings. The

methods of cold logic, hard facts, and critical distance from
the "object" of knowledge are increasingly seen in the same
light as polls, surveys, and government data: they are
designed to get the result the researchers want to get.[1] The
cultural imbalance is huge between the values attached to
modern "scientific" modes of thought, which has often been
the only game in town, and the cognitive capacities of our
spiritual and experiential life to "know" the truth and to be
set free by it.

The claims and techniques of skeptical detachment and
scientific disinterestedness are about as valid methods of
drawing forth knowledge about the world as the old oaken
bucket is useful in drawing up water. Postmodern theorists
are charting the course to a new "scientific method." The
modes of knowledge in this new "scientific method" are
more relational (less propositional), more experiential (less
experimental), more image-based (less word-centered) and
more celebratory and communal (less cerebral and individual).

A Christianity that is wedded to modern positivist arguments is a Christianity that is in trouble, and a Christianity
that ironically is in the clutches of relativism and subjectivism. The suffocating bell jar of modern science can bring
little air and still less fire to life. Or to switch metaphors, one
can beat the bush to death but fail to find the bird that hides
within.

The modern world became intellectually drunk on one
way of seeing. The truth is there are multiple ways of seeing the world. Perception is everything. As one physician
put it, "Your headache feels great to a druggist." Ironically,
one of the great "modern" achievements, *The Dictionary
of National Biography,* tacitly admits this. The DNB lists

two kinds of footnotes: the scholarly ones with full biblio-graphic apparatus, and the ones that say simply "personal knowledge."

There are at least two ways of knowing Shakespeare, the DNB implies. One is like the way Thomas Hardy said a fusspot friend knew Shakespeare: "He knew his Shakespeare to the dregs of the footnotes." The other way is through "personal knowledge" of Shakespeare and his life and times, a way scholars have admired mainly from a safe distance.

There are the same two ways of knowing Jesus.

✝ ✝ ✝

Why was it that his charm revealed
Somehow the surface of a shield?
        —Edwin Arlington Robinson, "Flamonde"[2]

✝ ✝ ✝

Modern science was largely autistic in relation to non-scientific modes of knowledge. The curriculum of knowledge that connects us to nature or to God was especially censured.

For example, there is more than a single way of "know-ing" a flower. One way (more Western, more modern) of "knowing" a flower is to be full of oneself, one's wits and wisdom, and to subject that flower to withering critique. This first way of "knowing" a flower is to experiment with it as something separate, to stand at a distance from it and pick it apart.

The other way (more biblical, more Eastern) of "know-ing" is really a way of "unknowing": to be "empty" of one-self and to let the flower reveal itself as it is. This second way of knowing a flower is to experience it, to enter in rather than stand back; to stand under (there is no ultimate understanding without standing under) and participate in its beauty. As A. E. Housman said, "to look at things in bloom/Fifty springs are little room."[3]

Knowledge by dissection analytically takes apart; knowledge by dance (gestures, smell, taste, touch, etc.) synthetically puts together.[4] In one you are rich—full of yourself. In one you are poor—empty of yourself. In one you are a distant observer or critic. In one you are an intimate lover. In the experimental you keep something at arm's-length distance; it is called critical detachment. In the experiential you put your arms around something; it is called loving embrace. In the words of music historian Nicholas Cook in his landmark study, "The very concept of 'really understanding' music becomes vacuous; there is only reading it, memorizing it, performing it, composing it, and listening to it—in short, loving it."[5]

Divine revelation has occurred. There are universal moral truths. Yet knowledge about these truths is socially constructed. We both discover and construct knowledge. God created our minds, even giving us some divine capacities. Thus God enabled us to perceive reality as well as to create new realities. We are both observer and participant at the same time.

Objectivity can no longer be the sole objective of the pursuit of truth.[6] Love can be as much a mode of knowledge as the old scientific method's detachment. To bring relatedness and separation together into an intimate-distance mode of discourse is at the heart of a participant-observer methodology.

In this E-P-I-C sense, a worshiper is both active and reflective, participating and observing, both in and out of the worship experience. You can't reflect without refracting. The promenade of worship is the ever dissolving and resolving dance between reflecting and refracting.

† † †

Many of us love religion all too much and God all too little. We love ourselves too much and the world too little.

—Mosaic (Los Angeles) pastor Erwin McManus

† † †

HARD SCIENCES

The second influence turning the church toward an E-P-I-C methodology is the hard sciences themselves. Indeed, most soft sciences have turned to the point of no return in their retreat from objective and subjective as archaic categories.[7] The whole field of culture studies is based on this notion of the observer as in some way a participant.[8] Some scholars are even being judged wanting for failing to mix participant-observer methodology with their scholarship.[9]

Chilean immunologist/biologist turned neuroscientist Francisco Varela once remarked that the hard sciences (laboratory-based) deal with the soft questions, and the soft sciences (clinical based) deal with the hard questions. But one of the hardest issues of life is the nature of truth.

Here science itself is pioneering a new "scientific method" and showing how the old "objective" pursuit of truth is not intellectually sound. The implications of this "new scientific method" for spirituality are monumental.

Too much of the new science (especially physics) is arguably being annexed as an outpost of the divine—a source of illumination into the ways of God. But it requires no stretch to state that the difference between classical physics and quantum mechanics or complexity physics is the difference between the scientist as an independent observer and the scientist as part of his or her own experiment, with one's very presence changing the course of events. By the time quantum theory was completed in the 1920s by Erwin Schrödinger, Max Born, and Paul Dirac, it was clear that the world was not independent of our observations. Nothing was apart from how it appeared, and nothing appeared except as it was observed.

✝ ✝ ✝

We do not see things as they are but as we are.
—Jewish proverb

✝ ✝ ✝

Let me give a smattering of examples from the hard sciences. Particle physicist Edwin Schrödinger states the new science paradigm eloquently: The world has not been given to us twice—once in spiritual or psychological terms and once in material terms. The world has been given once. The distinction between subjectivity and objectivity has been useful but specious.

When Thomas Kuhn wrote his classic text *The Structure of Scientific Revolutions* (1962), he was only embellishing what Albert Einstein and Karl Popper, in their ruminations on the course of scientific discovery, had already taught us. Both stressed that science advances not through the logic of induction or deduction but through imaginative leaps of faith.[10] A "paradigm shift" is an act of faith which creates new facts and new realities.

A moral methodology requires the frank acknowledgment of faith commitments. Value and faith commitments become rational parts of a scholar's scholarship, a seeker's search. Or as Canadian philosopher Lorraine Code puts it: "Subjectivity—however conflicted and multiple—becomes part of the conditions that make knowledge possible."[11] Subjectivity becomes a base of objectivity.[12] To be a scholar, or to be an ardent but not uncritical member of a faith community, is not antithetical. Postmodern intellectual integrity implies not methodological atheism but the methodological belief of a participant-observer. Every scientist plays both object and subject, resident and tourist, participant and observer.

Or as physicist Richard Feynman would put it, "To do science ya gotta have taste." And faith.

Even two of America's best-known mathematicians, Philip Davis and Reuben Hersh, have conceded that mathematics, properly understood, belongs in the humanities along with art, music, and literature.[13] Contemporary poet Robert Bly once read one of his poems, at the end of which he admitted that he had no idea what his concluding line meant. He only knew that the line belonged there, and one day the reason for it would be made manifest.

Physicist Fred Alan Wolf boils quantum physics down to this statement: "The universe does not exist independent of the thought of the observer," and "You will see it when you believe it."[14] How ironic to have awakened in a world where seeing is no longer believing. Believing is seeing.

Physicist John Wheeler has advised his colleagues to "cross out that old word 'observer' and replace it by the new word 'participator.'"[15] Erwin Schrödinger's famous cat-in-the-box experiment which reveals the pitfalls to "objective investigations"—where the cat is neither alive nor dead until the researcher opens the box, and the experimenter is intimately entangled in the experiment—have been reinforced by developments in game theory, which radically undermine confidence in simplistic notions of rationality.

French philosopher and phenomenologist Maurice Merleau-Ponty has scored telling arguments about the circularity between experience and world, science and experience, seeing and believing.[16] According to philosopher Nancey Murphy, "Changes in philosophical approaches in understanding causation, and changes in science itself, have in effect removed the major obstacles to belief in God's continuing action in the world. At the same time, these changes free us to pray expectantly. As a father is moved to act by the pleas of his children, Jesus tells us, so too is God moved to act by the pleas of his friends."[17]

The old scientific method still has its defenders, to be sure. Dennis Overbye in an influential essay argues that "science is nothing if not a spiritual undertaking," and that the spirituality of critical detachment "ennobles us."[18] So also developmental biologist Lewis Wolpert, who insists that science bears no responsibility for the technological applications of its work (i.e., nuclear bombs, biological weaponry, etc.).[19] For the late Carl Sagan, a human was "an astonishingly compact, self-ambulatory computer." That's it. In the deterministic world of modern science, prayer didn't make sense. And still doesn't for too many scientists.

But one of the untold and unknown stories of our time is the movement of the scientific community itself beyond the modern scientific method. One can see it manifested in British science writer Bryan Appleyard's protestations about "the appalling spiritual damage that science has done" by ignoring questions of meaning and purpose;[20] or scientist Donald A. Norman's laments over the spiritual and moral vacuum in which much of science is conducted.[21] Secular scientists like Carl Sagan, Freeman J. Dyson, Stephen Jay Gould have even invited a partnership with religion toward the end of "Preserving and Cherishing the Earth" in the aftermath of The Global Forum (1990).[22] Mary Midgley explores and explodes the claim that science makes religious faith unnecessary or anachronistic—or that science validates certain religious beliefs—or that science is itself a faith. In fact, Midgley castigates science for stealing our souls and leaving us without values.[23]

COGNITION THEORIES

The third set of influences pushing the church in E-P-I-C directions is the postmodern critique of the modern mind-set and especially the emergence of a new interdisciplinary matrix dedicated to the study of the mind called "cognitive sciences."

Historian John Lukacs calls "the mental intrusion into the structure of events" the most important fact of our time.[24] The field of cognition, which includes multiple academic disciplines of neuroscience, psychology, linguistics, genetics, computer science (especially artificial intelligence), anthropology, and philosophy, is generating new insights almost faster than they can be written down.

While some theologians whimper over the loss of modernity's fixed foundations and grounded reference points, scholars such as Humberto Maturana, Gregory Bateson, Heinz von Foerster, George Lakoff, Zenon W. Pylyshyn, Francisco Varela, Eleanor Rosch, and Michael Polanyi are showing how to live and move in an interdependent, relational mind-set, shifting our perspectives from control to flow, from abstract and disembodied reason to embodied and imaginative reason, from representation to participation, from literalism to metaphor, from fixed (or flexible) to fluid.[25]

Varela, an immunologist turned neuroscientist, is a radical critic of modern science's contention that our minds are nothing more than computers. In pursuit of that human creature so colorfully called "informavores,"[26] cognizers of cognition like Varela would put the soul into cognitive science. For them critical reason and "objective distance" give a very impartial account of how we humans know our world and ourselves.

Barbara McClintock, a geneticist who won the Nobel Prize in 1983 for her lifetime work on the genetics of corn, dissented from modern ways of knowing and suspended the boundaries between subject and object. For the scientist to understand, it meant "letting the experiment tell you what to do." She developed "a feeling for the organism," and told her biographer that things are "much more marvelous than the scientific method allows us to conceive." For her truth was as much hearing ("listening to the material") as seeing ("looking at hypotheses").[27]

† † †

You only see what you know.

—African proverb

† † †

The work in the biology of cognition done by Humberto R. Maturana and Francisco J. Varela has yielded unprecedented insights. It has shown that cognition is not simply a representation of the world out there but "an ongoing bringing forth of a world through the process of living itself." In the biological and systemic view of cognizing organisms, "Our experience is moored to our structure in a binding way."[28]

Varela insists on talking about an "observer-community" rather than an observer because "the knower is not the biological individual."[29] In other words an epistemology of participation extends in all directions, inward and outward, upward and downward. It involves, first, coming theoretically clean with one's point of view. No more charades: "As a historian, he is an atheist; as a professor, he is a polytheist; as a person, he is a Christian." It involves, second, paying homage to the varieties of conceptual repertory available, and recognizing that other conceptual systems have points of

view worth considering more than their charm as an unac-
customed vantage point.

Russian orthodox theologian Georges Florovsky argues
that all inquiry is "prejudiced" from the start—"prejudiced"
because every "cross-examination" or observation implies a
theoretical perspective. "Observation itself is impossible
without some interpretation, that is, understanding."[30]

E-P-I-C worship need not shelve our Enlightenment
inheritance of rational, linear worship. Nor need it stroke the
growing antirationalism that puffs up antirationality to a
virtue and demonizes reason, logic, and rules of evidence
almost to the status of a sin.[31] One need not leap from the
frying pan of the "disembodied observer" to the fire of a
"dis-worlded mind" wherein the mind constructs the world
on its own terms.[32] In his exploration of what reason hath
wrought in Western culture, Canadian novelist/historian
John Ralston Saul has demonstrated that the critique of the
dictatorship of reason doesn't mean the rejection of reason
or a thoroughly insouciant attitude toward "the facts."[33]

† † †

*The astronomical evidence leads to a biblical view of
the origin of the world.*
—Astronomer/religious agnostic Robert Jastrow[34]

† † †

We need to admit the problems of absolutist thinking
without giving up the belief in absolutes. There is no longer
"absolute space" or "absolute time" since Einstein. There is
no longer "absolute currency" since Nixon (who took the

U.S. off the gold standard in 1972). There is no longer "absolute sovereignty" since the collapse of nation states like the Soviet Union, etc. There is no longer "absolute . . ."

The examples are endless.

Yet the vanishing of absolutes does not mean the emergence of anarchy or relativism. Even without "absolute space" and "absolute time" one can still navigate space and time and reach the moon or a noon meeting. Even without "absolute currency" I can still buy groceries and our global syrup ("Coke"). Even without "absolute sovereignty" presidential campaigns are the biggest shows in town, and nations strut their political powers.

In a world of Cheshire-cat absolutes, one absolute remains absolute. That absolute is Jesus: the Way, the Truth, the Life, and a cornucopia of 117 other scriptural names like
The Bright Morning Star
The Dayspring from on High
The Sun of Righteousness
The Light of the World
The Lily of the Valley
The Rose of Sharon
The Bread of Life
The Door of the Sheepfold
The Good Shepherd
The Horn of Salvation
The Lamb of God
The Lion of Judah
The Root of David
The True Vine
The First Fruits
The Cornerstone of the Church
The Alpha and Omega
The Name Above All Names

Conclusion

In many Mediterranean cultures, beauty is more than an intellectual aesthetic. It is an aesthetic of experience, participation, images, and communal celebration. The French scholar Pierre Babin tells of seeing a number of Corsican elders sitting motionless under a tree, staring at a picturesque mountain range.

He spoke to the villagers "of the beauty of the landscape."

They responded: "We feel good here."

Babin, unsure whether they understood him properly, tried again: "Your village is beautiful!"

Once more they replied: "Do you feel good in our village?"

For them beauty was not fullness of artistry or perfection of lines. It was fullness of being and perfection of presence.[35]

An E-P-I-C epistemology does not negate objectivism with subjectivism in another recurring dualism. Rather, it encompasses both in a wider enfoldment that brings together organism and environment.[36] In an E-P-I-C epistemology rationality is expanded to include experience. The E-P-I-C perspective moves beyond objective and subjective "groundings" to an experiential accounting of truth where presence and participation play literally a "critical" role in history.

Philosopher Nancey Murphy was asked to address the question of "Does Prayer Make a Difference?" Her answer cuts to the chase at the running of the universe. "Apparently a great measure of the good in God's kingdom is our opportunity to participate in his work." Murphy then quotes P. T. Forsyth, a Scottish theologian writing early in this century, who suggested that God designed the universe in such a way that we participate in creating our world and our own experiences of God.

> "It is [God's] will—His will of grace—that prayer should prevail with Him and extract blessings."[37]

In other words, we both observe the world and worship the God who created everything in it. And at the same time we participate in creating God's world by creatively imaging God's ongoing creation as drivers of social change. I don't expect anyone (especially God) to agree with all my ideas (I have many, and as hard as I try, not all of them are under total subjection). But God has so structured the universe that we get to participate in God's ongoing creation as drivers of social change.

Observer-participant worship does not give up critical methods but rather places them within a larger matrix of reality of which they are only a part. In the paradoxical harmony of objective and subjective truth, there is opened up an intimate-distance way of knowing that is characterized by partnership in knowledge, not mastery of knowledge, and in which freedom and relationship do not cancel each other out but interpenetrate and help to create each other.

While a worship methodology that is more Experiential, Participative, Imaged-based, and Corrected will likely be classified as postmodern, its whole life and being inheres in the biblical tradition.[38] In fact, this is one area where the "postmodern" takes us "back to the future." For Jesus truth was not propositions or the property of sentences. Rather, truth was what was revealed through our participation and interaction with him, others, and the world.

But first one had to be freed up to receive those moments of truth being "unconcealed"[39] all around us.

First one had to be open to the revelatory events in which the divine disclosure presents itself in our everyday lives, beckoning us into more E-P-I-C forms of faith and worship.

First one had to be a follower of the E-P-I-C Original.

Faith Practices and Web Interactives

1. For an example of the "participant observation" method at work, read Robin M. *LeBlanc's Bicycle Citizens: The Political World of the Japanese Housewife* (Berkeley: University of California Press, 1999).

2. Watch the movie *Reality Bites* together as a group. It includes a valedictory address, where she concludes her speech with the following ending, to enthusiastic applause: "The answer is . . . I don't know the answer."

What is the significance of this ending? To what questions do we know the answers?

3. *Christianity Today* recently ran an interesting editorial. In the field of Christian fiction, it noted, stories are set either in the distant past or at the end of human history. The author raised the question of whether this might be symptomatic of the church's inability to find itself in the present.

What do you think?

4. What are the main sources of metaphors for what it means to be an American? Do you find any significance in the fact that fifteen million USAmericans visited Anaheim's Disneyland during 1997, while only 10.8 million visited the nation's capitol?[40]

5. Erwin McManus is the senior minister of a church in Los Angeles called Mosaic. McManus calls L.A. "the pregame warmup for the future culture we'll have to engage."[41] In talking about his ministry, he argues that "my goal is not necessarily to have a postmodern church. My goal is to have a biblical church that effectively reaches the postmodern context."

What is the distinction?

6. Rent the movie *The Blair Witch Project,* perhaps the most talked about movie of 1999. People usually either love the movie as an original masterpiece or hate it. Which one are you? Or do you occupy middle ground?

Visit its website *http://www.blairwitch.com.*

Are there E-P-I-C implications of this movie?

7. Apply what I call the "10 Year Rule" to your church. Look back ten years in time. Can you recognize your church? Are you basically the same church you were then? Or are you barely recognizable? When you compare where you are today with where you were ten years ago, if you can't say, "I don't recognize the place," you don't get it.

8. Listen to Gen-Xers discuss missions at the International Mission Board (IMB) website *www.imb.org.*

9. "We are all of us doomed to spend our lives watching a movie of our lives—we are always acting on what has just finished happening. It happened at least 1/30 of a second ago. We think we're in the present, but we aren't. The present we know is only a movie of the past, and we will really never be able to control the present through ordinary means. That lag has to be overcome some other way, through some kind of total breakthrough."[42]

Isn't the message of the gospel that the breakthrough we are looking for is the grace of Jesus Christ?

10. Does everything about the Old World Church spell ecclesiastical disintegration? Is there a sweet aroma to everything about The New World Churches? Or can these two aromas be found in both camps?

11. For a look at the postmodern transition from street level, visit *http://www.theooze.com*, my favorite Christian resource.

ENDNOTES

FOREWORD

1. David Lehman, "The Answering Stranger," *Operation Memory* (Princeton, N.J.: Princeton University Press, 1990), 20.
2. Romano Guardini, *The End of the Modern World* (Wilmington, Del.: Intercollegiate Studies Institute, 1998), 51. Romano Guardini (1885–1968) was professor of philosophy and theology at the University of Munich. His classic work *The End of the Modern World* was originally a set of lectures delivered at Tübingen in the winter session (1947–48) and then during the summer session at his own school, the University of Munich.
3. Romano Guardini, *The End of the Modern World,* Part II: Power and Responsibility (Wilmington, Del.: Intercollegiate Studies Institute, 1998), 118.
4. These are elaborated by Wesley K. Willmer and J. David Schmidt in *The Prospering Parachurch: Enlarging the Boundaries of God's Kingdom* (San Francisco: Jossey-Bass, 1998).

5. Roper Starch Worldwide Survey, "2004: A Personal Odyssey," *Fast Company*, September 1999, 262. *www.fastcompany.com/online/27/survey.html*

6. "Fast Talk: New Ideas for a New Medium," *Fast Company*, October 1999, 70.

7. My initial groundwork for an ancient-future methodology was laid in *Quantum Spirituality: A Postmodern Apologetic* (Dayton, Ohio: Whaleprints, 1991).

8. As elaborated most fully in my postmodern trilogy, *SoulTsunami: Sink or Swim in New Millennium Culture* (Grand Rapids, Mich.: Zondervan Publishing House,1999); *AquaChurch: Essential Leadership Arts for Piloting Your Church in Today's Fluid Culture* (Loveland, Colo.: Group, 1999); and *SoulSalsa* (Grand Rapids: Mich.: Zondervan Publishing House, 2000).

9. John R. W. Stott, *The Contemporary Christian: Applying God's Word to Today's World* (Downers Grove, Ill.: InterVarsity Press, 1992), 24–29.

10. Ibid., 29.

11. Ludwig Wittgenstein, *Culture and Value*, as quoted in H. L. Hix, *Spirits Hovering over the Ashes: Legacies of Postmodern Theory* (Albany: State University of New York Press, 1995), v.

12. Peter Marshall, *Riding the Wind: A New Philosophy for a New Era* (New York: Cassell, 1998), 7.

13. For more on these "leadership arts," see my *AquaChurch*.

14. Ninety-two percent of Southern Baptists will die without ever witnessing to another person about Jesus, argues one executive of the North American Mission Board. If it's that

high for Southern Baptists, think how high the figure must be for other tribes?

15. I love how René Girard puts it: the Gospels are "the essential text in the cultural upheaval of the modern world." See *Violent Origins: Walter Burkert, René Girard, and Jonathan Z. Smith on Ritual Killing and Cultural Formation*, ed. Robert G. Hammerton-Kelly (Stanford, Calif.: Stanford University Press, 1987), 141.

Introduction

1. Kirk Douglas, *The Broken Mirror: A Novella* (New York: Simon & Schuster, 1997); Kirk Douglas, *The Rag Man's Son* (New York: Simon & Schuster, 1998); Kirk Douglas, *Climbing the Mountain: My Search for Meaning* (New York: Simon & Schuster, 1997).

2. As referenced in J. Mack Stiles, *Speaking of Jesus: How to Tell Your Friends the Best News They Will Ever Hear* (Downers Grove, Ill.: InterVaristy Press, 1995), 120.

3. As quoted in Daniel McNeill, *The Face* (Boston: Little, Brown, 1998), 51.

4. For more see *www.kisshop.com.* Tom Shannon's *Goldmine's Price Guide to KISS Collectibles.* Kris Manty, "KISS & Tell," *Ebay Magazine* 1 (Premiere 1999), 96–97.

5. This is a euphemism for "kiss my—." The devil supposedly demands kisses on his behind.

6. Merlin Donald, "The Widening Gyre: Religion, Culture and Evolution," *Science & Spirit Magazine*, 10 (July/August 1999): 22–23. Check out *http://208.176.30.78/*

7. Nicolas James Perella, *The Kiss Sacred and Profane: An Interpretative History of Kiss Symbolism and Related Religio-Erotic Themes* (Berkeley: University of California Press, 1969), 1.

8. Roman law named an offense called *crimen osculationis*, or the crime of unchaste kissing—kissing someone against their will.

9. Bernard J. Hibbitts, "Coming to Our Senses: Communication and Legal Expression in Performance Cultures," *Emory Law Journal* 41 (1992): 933.

10. *Paed.*3.11. As quoted in William Klassen, "The Sacred Kiss in the New Testament," *New Testament Studies* 39 (1993): 134.

11. As quoted in Daniel McNeill, *The Face* (Boston: Little, Brown, 1998), 56.

12. John Nolland, *Luke 18:35–24:53*, Word Biblical Commentary, 35c (Dallas, Tex.: Word Books, 1993), 1088.

13. William Klassen, "The Sacred Kiss in the New Testament," *New Testament Studies* 39 (1993): 130.

14. Ibid., 128.

15. Ibid., 132–33.

16. Ibid., 135.

17. The Grand Inquisitor episode is in book 5, chapter 5. One of many editions is Fyodor Dostoevski, *The Brothers Karamazov*, tr. Constance Garnell (New York: Modern Library [n.d.]), 255–74.

18. See Aristotle, *De Anima in the Version of William of Moerbeke and the Commentary of St. Thomas Aquinas*, trans. Kenelm Foster and Silvester Humphries (London: Routledge and Kegan Paul, 1951), 185 (*Commentary* no. 260), 493–94 (*Text* no. 435).

19. Ashley Montagu, *Touching: The Human Significance of the Skin,* 3d ed. (New York: Harper & Row, 1986), 123.

20. Frederick Leboyer, *Loving Hands* (New York: Alfred A. Knopf, 1976), 16.

21. Joseph Chilton Pearce, *Magical Child: Rediscovering Nature's Plan for Our Children* (New York: E. P. Dutton, 1977), 53.

22. *HomeLife,* September 1998, 66.

23. Martha Pelaez-Nogueras, Tiffany M. Field, Ziarat Hossain, Jeffrey Pickens, "Depressed Mothers' Touching Increases Infants' Positive Affect and Attention in Still-Face Interactions," *Child Development,* 67 (August 1996): 1780–92.

24. Bernard J. Hibbitts, "Coming to Our Senses: Communication and Legal Expression in Performance Cultures," *Emory Law Journal* 41 (1992): 924.

25. Greg Campbell, as quoted in Mariana Caplan, *Untouched: The Need for Genuine Affection in an Impersonal World* (Prescott, Ariz.: Hohm Press, 1998), 159.

26. Tony Del Prete makes this case in "The Touchy Subject of Touching," *Education Digest,* 62 (March 1997) 59–61.

27. There are "contact cultures" (Arabs, Latin Americans, Southern Europeans), and there are "noncontact cultures" (Asians, North Americans, Northern Europeans).

28. George R. Beasley-Murray, *John,* Word Biblical Commentary, 36 (Waco, Tex.: Word Books, 1987), 376.

29. D. A. Carson, *The Gospel According to John* (Grand Rapids, Mich.: William B. Eerdmans, 1991), 641–42.

30. *Oxford Study Bible* contains a note that says, "Jesus' prohibition, *do not cling to me,* shows that Mary's gesture is premature, because his glorification is incomplete." See

Oxford Study Bible: Revised English Bible with the Apocrypha, ed. M. Jack Suggs, Katharine Doob Sakenfeld, James R. Mueller (New York: Oxford University Press, 1992), 1391.

31. Raymond Brown says that any comparison of this scene with that of Thomas is "irrelevant." I'm not so sure that one can so easily dismiss this problem of how to harmonize the two.

Here is how Brown resolves the problem:

> In telling her not to hold on to him, Jesus indicates that his permanent presence is not by way of appearance, but by way of the gift of the Spirit that can come only after he has ascended to the Father. . . . Instead of trying to hold on to Jesus (not, of course, that she could actually have prevented his ascension), she is commanded to go and prepare his disciples for that coming of Jesus when the spirit will be given.

"I am not yet ascended . . ." means that Jesus is in the process of ascending, after which he will give the Holy Spirit. When Jesus next appears to the disciples, he is glorified and gives them the Spirit. Mary sees him in the process of his ascending, and is told that she must relate to him differently (Raymond E. Brown, *The Gospel According to John*, Anchor Bible [Garden City, N.Y.: Doubleday, 1979], 1011–12, 1014).

32. For the eucharistic exploration of John 21, see Alan Shaw, "The Breakfast by the Shore and the Mary Magdalene Encounter as Eucharistic Narratives," *Journal of Theological Studies* 25 (April 1974): 12–26.

33. This language of the kiss of love as a "heartquake" comes from Lord Byron. "A long, long kiss, a kiss of youth and love/ . . . /Each kiss a heart-quake, for a kiss's strength."

See Canto 2, stanza 186 of Lord Byron, *Don Juan*, ed. T. G. Steffan (New Haven: Yale University Press, 1982), 148.

34. John Galt, *The Life, Studies, and Works of Benjamin West, Esq., President of the Royal Academy of London* (London: Printed for T. Cadell and W. Davies, Strand, 1820; repr. Gainesville, Fla.: Scholars' Facsimiles & Reprints, 1960), 9–10.

35. Mariana Caplan, *Untouched: The Need for Genuine Affection in an Impersonal World* (Prescott, Ariz.: Hohm Press, 1998), xix.

36. Mark Ward, "Body Gets the Message Across," *New Scientist* 152 (14 December 1996): 20.

CHAPTER ONE: E(xPERiENTiAL)-P-i-C

1. For the capturing of mainline Protestantism by the forces of modernization, see my article, "The 1960s: The Crisis of Liberal Christianity and the Public Emergence of Evangelism," in *Evangelism and Modern America*, ed. George Marsden (Grand Rapids, Mich.: William B. Eerdmans Publ. Co., 1984), 29–45.

2. Samuel L. Dunn, "Christianity's Future: The First-World Church Takes a Back Seat," *Futurist* 23 (March-April 1989): 34–37; Kim A. Lawton, "Faith Without Borders: How the Developing World is Changing the Face of Christianity," *Christianity Today*, 19 May 1997, 39, 42–49. This trend is evidenced by the proliferation of both Western and non-Western titles such as: William A. Dyrness, *Emerging Voices in Global Christian Theology* (Grand Rapids, Mich.: Zondervan Publ. House, 1994); Franklyn J.

Balasundarum, *Contemporary Asian Christian Theology* (Dehli: Indian Society for Promoting Christian Knowledge; John Parratt, *A Reader in African Christian Theology* (London: SPCK, 1987); and *Theology Cooked in an African Pot*, ed. Klaus Fiedler, Paul Gundani, and Hilary Mijoga, ATISCA Bulletin, 4–6 (1996/1997) (Zomba, Malawi: Association of Theological Institutions in Southern and Central Africa, 1998).

3. In these terms, the challenge facing mainline Protestantism can be stated simply: mainline Protestantism is basically denominational religion. And postmodern culture is postdenominational.

4. George Barna, "Teenagers and Their Relationships," *The Barna Report*, January-March 1999, 2. See also Barna Research Online, "Pastors and Laity Hold Divergent Views about Spiritual Revival," Press release, 27 October 1998, *http://207.198.84.9/cgi-bin/ PagePressRelease.asp?PressReleaseID=12*

5. Sandra Hofferth and Jack Sandberg, "Changes in American Children's Time, 1981–1997," Institute for Social Research, University of Michigan, as reported in Charles Fishman, "Smorgasbord Generation," *American Demographics*, 21 (May 1999), 58–59, http://www.demograpics.com/ publications/ ad/99_ad/ 9905_ad/ ad990501.htm

6. *Meister Eckhart, A Modern Translation* by Raymond Bernard Blakney (New York: Harper Torchbooks, 1941), 241.

7. Stewart Alsop, "Contemplating eBay's Funeral," *Fortune*, 7 June 1999, 201.

8. *Immanuel Kant's Critique of Pure Reason*, 2d ed., trans. Norman Kemp Smith (London: Macmillan, 1973), 41.

9. For more on this, see "Life Ring #6: Get EPIC" in my *SoulTsunami: Sink or Swim in the New Millennium Culture*

(Grand Rapids, Mich.: Zondervan, 1999), 185–235. For the fullest elaboration of this phenomenon, see B. Joseph Pines II and James H. Gilmore, *The Experience Economy: Work Is Theatre and Every Business Is a Stage* (Boston: Harvard Business School Press, 1999).

10. Mitch Albom, *Tuesdays with Morrie: An Old Man, a Young Man, and Life's Greatest Lesson* (New York: Doubleday, 1997), 61.

11. As quoted in Anna Muoio, ed., "Unit of One: Sales School," *Fast Company*, November 1998, 108. *http://www.fastcompany.com/online/19/one.html*

12. Lee Zalben, as quoted in Beth Gardiner, "Restauranteur Sticks with Peanut Butter," Associated Press Release, 24 February 1999, *http://www.messenger-inquirer.com/food/e27890.htm*.

13. Tom Beaudoin, *Virtual Faith: The Irreverent Spiritual Quest of Generation X* (San Francisco: Jossey-Bass, 1998), 78.

14. Michael J. Wolf, "The Pleasure Binge," *Wired*, March 1999, 86. http://www.wired.com/wired/archive/7.03/entertain.html

15. Cheryl Russell, "The New Consumer Paradigm," *American Demographics*, April 1999, 54.

16. Ibid.

17. "Perspectives," *Newsweek*, 25 October 1999, 25. http://newsweek.com/nw-srv/issue/17_99b/printed/us/dept/pe/pe.htm

18. Quoted in Lucy McCauley, "Measure What Matters," *Fast Company*, May 1999, 111. *http://www.fastcompany.com/online/24/0ne.html*

19. Worldwide $1.9 trillion is spent annually on tourism. See Peter Weber, "It Comes Down to the Coasts," *World Watch*, March-April 1994, 21.

20. Lunar hotels will specialize in people wanting to make love in one-sixth the gravity of planet Earth, according to one futurist who spends an entire chapter on this feature of the future. "One of the great joys of the twenty-first century will be taking holidays in lunar hotels for the specific purpose of making love, and of describing the experience afterwards." See chapter 12 "Building Selenopolis" in Adrian Berry, *The Next 500 Years: Life in the Coming Millennium* (New York: W. H. Freeman, 1996), 153–164, 156.

21. NASA has already issued contracts for two research vehicles, the X-33 and X-34, to test the technology for an airplane-like launcher.

22. Michael J. Wolf, "The Pleasure Binge," *Wired*, March 1999, 89.

23. The cover theme was called "Choosing My Religion." See John McManus, "The Soul Connection," *American Demographics*, April 1999, 6.

24. Lisa Gubernick with Philippe Mao, "The Happiness Hucksters," *Forbes*, 9 October 1995, 83. The figure for 1995 was estimated at $1.6 billion.

25. As quoted in Bruce Horovitz, "'90s Luxury Beyond Top of the Line." *USA Today*, 6 July 1999, 2A.

26. See Andrew Ballantyne, "The View from Lansdown Towers" [Review of Timothy Mowl, *William Beckford: Composing for Mozart* (London: John Murray, 1998)], *TLS: Times Literary Supplement*, 18 September 1998, 20.

27. "The percentage of teenagers attending weekly services has dropped from 55 percent in 1986 to 42 percent in 1997. Meanwhile, teens express rising belief in angels and astrology." From George Gallop, "The Religious Life of Young People," as reported in Richard Cimino and Don Lattin,

"Choosing My Religion," *American Demographics*, April 1999, 64.

28. For this quote and his investigation of healing practices, see Chip Brown, *Afterwards, You're a Genius: Faith, Medicine, and the Metaphysics of Healing* (New York: Riverhead Books, 1998), 328–29.

29. George Barna, "One Out of Three Adults Is Now Unchurched," news release, 25 February 1999. Of these "unchurched," two out of three call themselves "Christian," and one-third claim they have a personal commitment to Jesus. Check out this Web site:
http://207.198.84.9/cgi-bin/PagePressRelease.asp?PressReleaseID=18

30. "The Unchurched," *The Alabama Baptist*, 1 July 1999, 16.

31. Susan Mitchell, *American Generations: Who They Are, How They Live, What They Think* (Ithaca, N.Y.: New Strategist Publications, 1998), 75.

32. I want to thank my doctoral student Kenneth L. Ray for this insight.

33. Polly Labarre, "Unit of One: What's New, What's Not," *Fast Company*, January 1999, 74.
http://www.fastcompany.com/online/21/one.html

34. Seth Zuckerman has held this title since 1997 for Ecotrust, a Portland, Oregon based environmental group. See *News and Views*,
http://www.explorecbd.org/newsviews/nv_zuckerman1.html

35. Now CEO of garage.com. See Guy Kawasaki and Michele Moreno, *Rules for Revolutionaries: The Capitalist Manifesto for Creating and Marketing New Products and Services* (New York: HarperBusiness, 1999).

36. Geoffrey Colvin, "How to Be a Great ECEO," *Fortune*, 24 May 1999, 104–10, quotes on 104, 107.

37. See Michael Slaughter, *Out on the Edge: A Wake-up Call for Church Leaders on the Edge of the Media Reformation* (Nashville: Abingdon Press, 1998); Len Wilson, *The Wired Church: Making Media Ministry* (Nashville: Abingdon Press, 1999); Kim Miller, *Multi-Sensory Worship* (Nashville: Abingdon Press, 1999).

38. This happened during its 1998 season. Among the smells? Raw meat and flatulence.

39. Jane Miller, *Seductions: Studies in Reading and Culture* (Cambridge, Mass.: Harvard University Press, 1991), 151.

40. Robert Rabbin, *Invisible Leadership: Igniting the Soul at Work* (Lakewood, Colo.: Awakening/Acropolis Books, 1998), xxv.

41. Anne A. Simpkinson, "A Woman of Faith," *Common Boundary* 17 (May/June 1999): 33.

42. In his public lectures, biblical scholar John Dominic Crossan prefers to call the "Enlightenment" the "Endarkenment."

43. Barna Research Online, "Experiencing Worship," *http://207.198.84.9/cgi-bin/PageCategory.asp*

44. See Donald S. Whitney, "Unity of Doctrine and Devotion," in *The Compromised Church: The Present Evangelical Crisis*, ed. John H. Armstrong (Wheaton, Ill: Crossway Books, 1998), 242, where he calls these experiences "Scripture-inaugurated."

45. Paul Crichton, "A Prescription for Happiness? Finding Limits to the Use of Antidepressants," *TLS: Times Literary Supplement*, 2 July 1999, 14.

46. See especially John Milbank, Catherine Pickstock, and Graham Ward, ed., *Radical Orthodoxy: A New Theology* (New York: Routledge, 1999). See also John Milbank, *The*

Word Made Strange: Theology, Language, Culture (Cambridge, Mass.: Blackwell Publishers, 1997) and John Milbank, *Theology and Social Theory* (Oxford: Blackwell Publishers, 1990).

47. See the work of novelist and theologian Michael Riddell, *Threshold of the Future: Reforming the Church in the Post-Christian West* (London: SPCK, 1998); Michael Riddell, *God's Home Page* (Oxford: Bible Reading Fellowship, 1998).

48. I first used this phrase in the early '90s. See my *FaithQuakes* (Nashville: Abingdon Press, 1994), 19. See also Robert Webber, *AncientFuture Faith: Rethinking Evangelicalism for a Postmodern Church* (Grand Rapids, Mich.: Baker Book House, 1999).

49. With thanks to inventor/entrepreneur/Atari founder Nolan Bushnell.

50. John Lennon and Paul McCartney, "All You Need is Love," *All You Need Is Love*,
http://www.qbc.clic.net/~dany/beatles/cha_xx00/chansons/aynil_tb.htm

51. Elaine Shepherd, *R. S. Thomas: Conceding an Absence: Images of God Explored* (New York: St. Martin's Press, 1996), 155.

52. William M. Easum, "Warning! Turning a Church Around Is a Dangerous Calling," *Net Results*, September 1999, 21.

53. Carlyle Murphy, "God Speaks from Above with Humor, Admonition," *Washington Post*, 8 July 1999, B1.

54. With thanks to Hal Brady, Unpublished sermon, "What about the Signs?" 11 July 1999, St. Luke United Methodist Church, Columbus, Georgia.

55. Bill Owens, *The Magnetic Music Ministry: Ten Productive Goals* (Nashville: Abingdon, 1995), 19–20.

56. William A. Beckham, *The Second Reformation: Reshaping the Church for the Twenty-First Century* (Houston, Tex.: Touch Publications, 1997), 130.

57. Dietrich Bonhoeffer, *Life Together*, trans. Daniel W. Bloesch, Dietrich Bonhoeffer Works, 5 (Minneapolis: Fortress Press, 1996), 47.

CHAPTER TWO: E-P(PARTICIPATORY)-I-C

1. See the work of two management consultants, Patricia McLagan and Christo Nel, *The Age of Participation: New Governance for the Workplace and the World* (San Francisco: Berrett-Koehler, 1995).

2. Lawrence M. Friedman, *The Horizontal Society* (New Haven: Yale University Press, 1999).

3. Walter Shapiro, "The New Lingua Franca," *American Demographics*, April 1999, 48. One of the new trends in the legal world is to represent yourself in court. "In two-thirds of all California domestic-relations cases, someone acts as their own attorney."

4. Just as writing was once the province of the few, and now almost everyone can write, so programming computers to do what you want them to do will one day be the privilege of the masses. Use a spreadsheet? You're a programmer. So argues Michael L. Dertouzos, *What Will Be: How the New World of Information Will Change Our Lives* (San Francisco: HarperEdge, 1997), 267.

5. There are fewer "professionals" as more people are becoming their own online stockbrokers. In an astonishing figure, almost half of U.S. households have become stockholders.

6. The sixty-year-old *Gourmet* magazine has totally revamped itself around this philosophy that we're all gourmets, not just a few old, fat, rich, white men.

7. Check out amazon.com's readers' reviews of J. K. Rowling's *Harry Potter and the Sorcerer's Stone*. As of 28 November 1999 there were 1,860 of them.

8. *USA Today* editorial, "A Defining Moment for Women's Sports," 12 July 1999, A16.

9. In 1988, there was $18.7 million in U.S. sales of karaoke products. Within five years the sales of karaoke hardware and software totaled $5 billion worldwide, $145.4 million in the USAmerica alone. See "A Strong Urge to Sing," *USA Today*, 30 September 1994, 1D.

10. Rush Limbaugh has a weekly audience of twenty million people.

11. Those who use the Web are more likely than the general USAmerican population to snorkel and skin-dive (4.2% to 2.29%); surf and windsurf (1.34% to 0.85%); downhill ski (6.55% to 3.68%); cross-country ski (2.75% to 1.58%); scuba dive (2.64% to 1.52%); white-water raft (2.44% to 1.44%); water-ski (3.86% to 2.36%); in-line skate (7.44% to 4.56%); snowboard (1.63% to 1.0%); racquetball (2.96% to 1.83%); mountain bike (6.07% to 3.86%); drive SUVs (13.21% to 8.45%). MRI New Media, as cited in "When They're Not on the Net . . . ," *American Demographics*, April 1999, 25.

12. See for example *Ultima,* first released in 1985.

13. Rachel X. Weissman, "Connecting with Digital Kids," *American Demographics*, April 1999, 16. *http://www.demographics.com/publications/ad/9904_ad/ad990405d.htm*

14. Ibid.

15. Southern Baptist pastor and freelance author Jim L. Wilson uses this phrase in his as yet unpublished article on the "cyber-pastor."

16. Charles Platt, "Interactive Entertainment," *Wired*, September 1995, 147. http://www.wired.com/wired/archive/ 3.09/interactive.html?topic=&topic_set=

17. Morgan Murphy, "The Chop Shop in Stuttgart," *Forbes*, 22 March 1999, 172.

18. Edwin Schlossberg, *Interactive Excellence: Defining and Developing New Standards for the Twenty-first Century* (New York: Ballantine, 1998), 81.

19. This draws heavily on McLagan & Nel, *The Age of Participation,* xiii.

20. Al Ries and Jack Trout, *Marketing Warfare* (New York: New American Library, 1986), 138.

21. Michael J. Wolf, "The Pleasure Binge," *Wired*, March 1999, 90. http://www.wired.com/wired/archive/7.03/ entertain.html?pg=1&topic=&topic_set=

22. Sandra Hofferth and Jack Sandberg, "Changes in American Children's Time, 1981–1997," Institute for Social Research, University of Michigan, as reported in Charles Fishman, "Smorgasbord Generation," *American Demographics* 21 (May 1999), 58–59. http://www.demographics.com/ publications/ad/99_ad/9905_ad/ad990501.htm

23. As cited in "Periscope: Vital Stats: 'I Prefer My Stars to Be Interactive,'" *Newsweek*, 30 August 1999, 10. *http://newsweek.com/nw-srv/issue/09_99b/printed/*

us/dept/ps/ps_2.htm

24. The bride and groom pull a name from a hat among the guests present. The bride and groom promise to imitate in their kiss however the named couple kisses. The kisses often range from light pecking to demonstrative, performative kisses.

25. An announcement is made that all those suitors who've been given keys to the bride's apartment must now turn them in. The plants come forward from throughout the reception hall, with a story told by each one, and the best man counts them. One is missing. After much cajoling, it is usually the rector/priest/pastor who reluctantly brings the last key up to the front.

26. Lisa Carlson, *Caring for the Dead: Your Final Act of Love* (Hinesburg, Vt.: Upper Access, 1998), esp. 9–11, 60–71, 99–100, 130, and the final section of the book which lists rules and regulations for each of the fifty states. See also *www.funerals.org/famsa*.

27. William W. George, chair and CEO of Medtronics, "Leadership: Building a Mission-Driven, Values-Centered Organization," *Vital Speeches*, 1 May 1999, 438–41.

28. Paul Roberts, "Total Teamwork: The Mayo Clinic," *Fast Company*, April 1999, 153. http://www.fastcompany.com/online23/totteam.html

29. Andrew Ford, "Illegal Harmony," interview with John Cage in Andrew Ford, *Composer to Composer,* 71.

30. Andrew Ford, "The Silences," interview with David Lumsdaine, in Andrew Ford, *Composer to Composer: Conversations about Contemporary Music* (London: Quartet Books, 1993), 71.

31. Lawrence W. Cheek, "Day to Day Department: These Trying Times," *SPA*, May/June 1999, 22.

32. "Reality Checks on the Road to Interactivity: Engines Blazing, Miles to Go," *John Naisbitt's Trend Letter*, 13 (23 June 1994): 2.

33. As quoted in Anna Muoio, ed., "Unit of One: The Art of Smart," *Fast Company*, July-August 1999, 102. http://www.fastcompany.com/online/26/one.html

34. Richard DeGrandpre, *Ritalin Nation: Rapid-fire Culture and the Transformation of Human Consciousness* (New York: W. W. Norton, 1999), 177. See also Lawrence H. Diller, *Running on Ritalin: A Physician Reflects on Children, Society, and Performance in a Pill* (New York: Bantam, 1998).

35. "Ritalin is no more an effective medical treatment than ADD is a valid medical disorder," contends Richard DeGrandpre, *Ritalin Nation: Rapid-fire*, 215.

36. For example the Biltmore Estate in Asheville, North Carolina, which includes the Vanderbilt family's 250-room mansion and the new Inn at Biltmore, which provides guest activities similar to what the Vanderbilt's would have offered their guests. *http://www.biltmore.com/inn.html*

37. See my *Quantum Spirituality: A Postmodern Apologetic* (Dayton, Ohio: Whaleprints, 1991).

38. One of the best examples of this is what Group Publishing did with my *AquaChurch* (Loveland, Colo.: Group Publishing, 1999).

39. I learned this word from children's author Dr. Mary Manz Simon.

40. See Eric Stanford, "Publishing for Postmoderns: An Introduction for Authors, Editors, and Publishers,"

(Colorado Springs, Colo.: Stanford Creative Services, 1999, 5.) Available from the author at *eric@stanfordcreative.com*.

41. Edward Gilbreath, "Why Pat Boone Went 'Bad,'" *Christianity Today*, 43 (4 October 1999): 62.

42. Pentecostalism boasts about twenty million new members a year, with especially large gains in Asia and Africa. Some Latin American countries are approaching Pentecostal majorities. Theologian Harvey Cox wrote his study of Pentecostalism not as an objective observer but as a participant. See Harvey Cox, *Fire from Heaven: The Rise of Pentecostal Spirituality and the Reshaping of Religion in the Twenty-first Century* (Reading, Mass.: Addison-Wesley, 1995).

43. See Tex Sample, *The Spectacle of Worship in a Wired World: Electronic Culture and the Gathered People of God* (Nashville: Abingdon Press, 1998).

44. As quoted in Charles Platt, "Interactive Entertainment," *Wired*, September 1995, 195. *http://www.wired.com/wired/archive/3.09/interactive.html?topic=&topic_set=*

45. Donald E. Messer, "Building Bridges Under Icy Waters," *Circuit Rider*, 19 (November 1995): 4.

46. Edwin Schlossberg, *Interactive Excellence: Defining and Developing New Standards for the Twenty-first Century* (New York: Ballantine, 1998), 40–41.

47. For more see Rachel X. Weissman, "Connecting with Digital Kids," 17.

48. Ibid.

49. Janet Horowitz Murray, *Hamlet on the Holodeck: The Future of Narrative in Cyberspace* (New York: Free Press. 1997), 97–182, esp. 98–99, 126, 154. In digital culture, change invites itself, which is at the heart of "transformation."

Or in Murray's words, "Because digital objects can have multiple instantiations, they call forth our delight in variety itself" (154).

50. PTA's declined from 12.1 million members in 1962 to 6.5 million in 1996.

51. See Mark Frauenfelder, "Gross National Product: Xtreme Candy Gets Real," *Wired*, June 1999, 212. who argues that "kids obviously like Warheads in large part because adults hate them. . . . They're also a favored medium for tribal bonding, a social lubricant" (211). *http://www.wired.com/wired/archive/7.06/ candy.html?pg=1&topic=&topic_set=*

52. Charles Arn, *How to Start a New Service: Your Church Can Reach New People* (Grand Rapids, Mich.: Baker Books, 1997), 167.

53. Ibid., 168.

54. As far as I know, this is the only program of its kind sponsored by a denomination—in this case, the Office of Communication (Louisville, Ky.) of the General Assembly Council of the Presbyterian Church (USA) and the Presbyterian Media Mission (Pittsburgh, Pa.). To learn more about this project contact John C. R. Silbert at *jsilbert@pcusa.org.*

Chapter Three: E-P-I(mage driven)-C

1. As quoted by D. J. Enright, *Interplay: A Kind of Commonplace Book* (New York: Oxford University Press, 1995), 152.

2. Emily Brontë, *Wuthering Heights*, ed. Hilda Marsden and Ian Jack (Oxford: Clarendon Press, 1976), 99.

3. For examples of this, see Bernard J. Hibbitts, "Making Sense of Metaphor: Visuality, Aurality, and the Reconfiguration of American Legal Discourse," *Cardozo Law Review* 16 (1994): 234.

4. With thanks to Kate Walker, president of Trimtab Communications, Seattle, Washington, for this reference.

5. Mark Twain as quoted in
http//www.epigraphics.com/mtwain.htm.

6. See linguist George Lakoff's and philosopher Mark Johnson's *Metaphors We Live By* (Chicago: University of Chicago Press, 1980), 40.

7. Ibid., 22.

8. Ibid., 125.

9. Ibid., 235.

10. Bob Kaufman, "$$Abomus Craxioms$$," *Solitudes Crowded with Loneliness* (New York: New Directions Publishing House, 1965), 80.

11. For more on this, see my "Can You Hear the Double Ring?" *Vital Ministry* 2 (March/April 1999): 34–37, and *SoulTsunami: Sink or Swim in New Millennium Culture* (Grand Rapids, Mich.: Zondervan Publishing House, 1999), 27–29.

12. For additional information, see The Garden's Web page: *http://www.the-garden.org/.*

13. James C. Collins and Jerry I. Porras, *Built to Last: Successful Habits of Visionary Companies* (New York: HarperBusiness, 1994), 212–18.

14. As reported in "NB," *TLS: Times Literary Supplement,* 23 May 1997, 14. For the actual quote see Fredric Jameson, *Signatures of the Visible* (New York: Routledge, 1990), 1.

15. Rob Wilson, "Cyborg America: Policing the Social Sublime in *Robocop* and *Robocop 2," The Administration of Aesthetics: Censorship, Political Criticism, and the Public Sphere,* ed. Richard Burt (Minneapolis: University of Minnesota Press, 1994), 290.

16. Peter Marshall, *Riding the Wind: A New Philosophy for a New Era* (New York: Cassell, 1998), 6.

17. Erwin R. McManus, "Engaging the Third Millennium," *Shout* 2 (Winter 1998): 4–5.

18. Wilfrid Mellers, *Between Old Worlds and New: Occasional Writings on Music* (Madison, N.J.: Fairleigh Dickinson University Press, 1997), 21.

19. "The Colorado School Slayings," *New York Times* editorial, 22 April 1999, A30.

20. Robert Rabbin, *Invisible Leadership: Igniting the Soul at Work* (Lakewood, Colo.: Awakening/Acropolis Books, 1998), 118–19.

21. See Stephen Prince, *Savage Cinema: Sam Peckinpah and the Rise of Ultraviolent Movies* (Austin: University of Texas Press, 1998), where the author tries to make a case for the legitimacy of violent images and "the unfortunate tradition of movie violence that they have helped inspire" (xvi).

22. As quoted in Robert Rabbin, *Invisible Leadership,* 20.

23. See the most recent Cassandra Report from Youth Intelligence, as referenced in Lisa Goff, "Don't Miss the Bus!" *American Demographics,* 21 (August 1999), 53.

24. Sallie McFague TeSelle, *Speaking in Parables: A Study in Metaphor and Theology* (Philadelphia: Fortress Press, 1975), 56.

25. Wes Nisker, *Crazy Wisdom* (Berkeley, Calif.: Ten Speed Press, 1990; reprint 1999). Also available as Audio Cassette (Berkeley, Calif.: Audio Literature, 1992).

26. As quoted in William C. Taylor, "Whatever Happened to Globalization?" *Fast Company*, September 1999, 231. *http://www.fastcompany.com/online/27/sorrell.html.*

CHAPTER FOUR, E-P-İ-C(oNNECTED)

1. So argues Joseph Epstein, "Move It on Down," *TLS: Times Literary Supplement*, 23 July 1999, 27.

2. Daniel Yankelovich, *The Magic of Dialogue: Transforming Conflict into Cooperation* (New York: Simon & Schuster, 1999), 217.

3. As quoted in Edward M. Hallowell, *Connect* (New York: Pantheon Books, 1999), 15.

4. Myra Stark, senior vice president of Consumer Insights at Saatchi and Saatchi.

5. As quoted in Daniel Roth, "Meg Muscles eBay Uptown," *Fortune*, 5 July 1999, 81–82.

6. Nicholas Boyle, *Who Are We Now? Christian Humanism and the Global Market from Hegel to Heaney* (Notre Dame, Ind.: University of Notre Dame Press, 1998), 305.

7. The church needs "to listen more clearly to people's inner spiritual journeys and religious experiences . . . and to help them build on those experiences." See Princeton Religion

Research Center, *The Unchurched American: 10 Years Later* (Princeton, N.J.: Princeton Religion Research Center, 1988), 4.

8. In 1996, AOL opened Love@AOL where a few hundred personal ads were placed as part of the Valentine's Day celebration. Three years later there were more than 125,000 personal ads year round, with 23,000 coming from people ages twenty-one to twenty-five and another 20,000 from those eighteen to twenty. George Barna has discovered that the Internet is more of a friendship vehicle for black teenagers than for whites. [George Barna, "Teenagers and Their Relationships," *The Barna Report*, January-March 1999, 10; issued as an 8 July 1988 Press Release, *http://207.198.84.9/cgi-bin/ PagePressRelease.asp?PressReleaseID=21.*]

9. Greg Sandow, "An Orchestra That Lets Loose," *Wall Street Journal*, 21 September 1999, A24.

10. Order Trust CEO Jim Danielle, as quoted in David Dorsey, "The People Behind the People Behind E-Commerce," *Fast Company*, June 1999, 186. See also the AP report by Jim Salter on the St. Louis Galleria, "Mall Battles Internet for Sales," *The Register-Guard* (Eugene-Springfield, Oreg.), 25 November 1999, F1.

11. Elizabeth Weise, "Net Use Doubling," *USA Today*, 16 April 1998, 1A.

12. Norman H. Nie, "Tracking Our Techno-Future," *American Demographics*, July 1999, 50. *http://www.demographics.com/publications/ ad/99_ad/9907_ad/ad990707.htm.*

13. Ibid., 51.

14. Quoted in Edward M. Hallowell, *Connect* (New York: Pantheon Books, 1999), 19.

15. As quoted by Lawrence Cunningham, "Spirituality: Encountering Images of Christ," in Francis A. Eigo, ed., *Imaging Christ: Politics, Art, Spirituality* (Villanova, Pa.: Villanova University Press, 1991), 60.

16. As referenced by Gary Gardner, "Shared Destinies," *Utne Reader*, November-December 1999, 83.

17. Geoffrey Hill, *The Triumph of Love* (Boston: Houghton Mifflin, 1998), 46. Hill has been hailed as "the finest British poet of our time." His Christian musings have been called "the major achievement of late 20th century verse."

18. Tom Beaudoin, *Virtual Faith: The Irreverent Spiritual Quest of Generation X* (San Francisco: Jossey-Bass, 1998), 10.

19. Edward M. Hallowell, *Connect* (New York: Pantheon Books, 1999).

20. Ibid., 5.

21. Ibid., 4.

22. Ibid., especially chapter 19.

23. George Barna, "Teenagers and Their Relationships," *The Barna Report*, January-March 1999, 3.

24. Most USAmerican corporations have already jettisoned their heavily planned, centralized, and hierarchical apparatus for what are called "internal markets" and "intrapreneurs." See William E. Halal, "Let's Turn Organizations into Markets!" *The Futurist*, May-June 1994, 9, 13.

25. Of course, this assumes equivalent-diameter samples are compared.

26. The actual Latin is *Non coerceri maximo, contineri tamen a minimo, divinum est*, as cited by Joseph Ratzinger, *Introduction to Christianity* (San Francisco: Ignatius Press, 1990), 101.

27. As told by NEA President Bob Chase in "Education's Brave New World," *Vital Speeches*, 1 May 1999, 433.

28. With thanks to Robert Rabbin for first pointing this out. See his *Invisible Leadership: Igniting the Soul at Work* (Lakewood, Colo.: Awakening/Acropolis Books, 1998), 103–04.

29. As quoted in Steve Silberman, "Mystery Man," *Wired*, October 1999, 235. *http://www.wired.com/wired/archive/7.10/miller.html*.

30. Stephen Crites, "The Narrative Quality of Experience," *Journal of the American Academy of Religion* 39 (1971): 291–311.

31. See Mark Turner's *The Literary Mind* (New York: Oxford University Press, 1996).

32. As quoted in Mark Amory, "Elegy and Regret," (Review of John Betjeman, *Coming Home* [London: Methuen, 1997], in *TLS: Times Literary Supplement*, 21 November 1997), 9.

33. Thomas E. Boomershine, *Story Journey: An Invitation to the Gospel as Storytelling* (Nashville: Abingdon Press, 1988), 18.

34. Ibid., 17.

35. Huston Smith in Marilyn Snell, "The World of Religion According to Huston Smith," *Mother Jones*, November/December 1997, 43.

36. The analogy is that of Ram Dass, as cited by Huston Smith, in Snell, ibid.

37. Kenda Creasy Dean, Ron Foster, and Rita Collett, *The Godbearing Life: The Art of Soul Tending for Youth Ministry* (Nashville: Upper Room Books, 1998), 93.

38. Tony Alessandra and Michael J. O'Connor, *The Platinum Rule: Discover the Four Basic Business*

Personalities—and How They Can Lead You to Success (New York: Warner Books, 1996).

39. David and Tom Gardner, *The Motley Fool's Rule Breakers, Rule Makers: The Foolish Guide to Picking Stocks* (New York: Simon & Schuster, 1999). Also available on audiocassette (New York: Simon & Schuster, 1999).

40. Marcus Buckingham and Curt Coffman, *First, Break All the Rules: What the World's Greatest Managers Do Differently* (New York: Simon & Schuster, 1999).

41. This is the argument of Richard Firth Green's important study: *A Crisis of Truth: Literature and Law in Ricardian England* (Philadelphia: Pennsylvania University Press, 1999), xiv and ch. 1, "From Troth to Truth," 1–40.

42. H. R. Mackintosh, as quoted in Josiah Royce, *The Problem of Christianity: Lectures Delivered at the Lowell Institute in Boston and at Manchester College, Oxford* (New York: Macmillan, 1913) 2:331–32.

43. John Buchanan, "Give Me That Old Time Religion," Fourth Presbyterian Church, Chicago, 25 April 1999.

44. The definition is that of the National Congress for Community Economic Development, the trade association for community-based development organizations. For more information, see *http://www.ncced.org*

45. As related by John A. Huffman Jr., "Healing Power," St. Andrew's Presbyterian Church, Newport Beach, California, 8 November 1998.

46. *The Writings of George Washington from the Original Manuscript Sources 1745–1799,* ed. John C. Fitzpatrick (Washington: United States Government Printing Office, 1938), 27:254.

47. J. Leslie Houlden, "Teaching of the Book," *TLS: Times Literary Supplement*, 5 February 1999, 29.

48. "Fixed Prices: Going, Going, Gone," *Trend Letter: A Report on the Forces Transforming the Economy, Business, Technology, Society and the World* 18 (15 April 1999): 3.

49. Dietrich Bonhoeffer, *Life Together*, trans. Daniel W. Bloesch, Dietrich Bonhoeffer Works, 5 (Minneapolis: Fortress Press, 1954), 31.

ENDTRODUCTION

1. See especially Cynthia Crossen, *Tainted Truth: The Manipulation of Fact in America* (New York: Simon & Schuster, 1994). For the "statistical" relationship between Baptists and boozers, see Stephen Jay Gould, "The Smoking Gun of Eugenics," *Natural History*, December 1991, 8: "Do Baptist preachers cause public drunkenness? I raise this unlikely inquiry because an old and famous tabulation clearly shows a strong positive correlation between the number of preachers and the frequency of arrests for inebriation during the second half of the nineteenth century."

2. Edwin Arlington Robinson, "Flammonde," *A Little Treasury of American Poetry: The Chief Poets from Colonial Times to the Present Day*, ed. Oscar Williams (New York: Charles Scribner's Sons, 1952), 262.

3. A. E. Housman, "Loveliest of Trees, the Cherry Now," *A Shropshire Lad* (New York: Illustrated Editions Co., 1932), 17.

4. See Martha Heyneman, *The Breathing Cathedral: Feeling Our Way into a Living Cosmos* (San Francisco: Sierra Club Books, 1993).

5. Nicholas Cook, *Music, Imagination, Culture* (New York: Oxford University Press, 1990), 186.

6. Daphne Patai, "Sick and Tired of Scholars' Nouveau Solipsism," *Chronicle of Higher Education*, 23 February 1994, A52.

7. Frank T. Birtel's essay "Choosing God and Choosing Man: A Post-Modern Challenge," *Reasoned Faith: Essays on the Interplay of Faith and Reason*, ed. Frank T. Birtel (New York: Crossroad, 1993), 160.

8. John Frow, *Cultural Studies and Cultural Value* (Oxford: Clarendon Press, 1995), 3.

9. See Albert Weale, "Old Nick in the Rain Forest," Review of Tony Brenton's *The Greening of Machiavelli: The Evolution of International Environmental Politics* (London: Earthscan Publications, 1994), *TLS: Times Literary Supplement*, 9 September 1994, 6.

10. See Karl Popper, *The Logic of Scientific Discovery* (New York: Harper Torchbooks, 1968), 458. For Thomas Kuhn see his *Structure of Scientific Revolutions* (Chicago: University of Chicago Press, 1962).

11. Lorraine Code, "Who Cares? The Poverty of Objectivism for a Moral Epistemology," in "Rethinking Objectivity II," ed. Allan Megill, *Annals of Scholarship* 9:1–2 (1992), 7.

12. See ibid., 6, where she points to "both the subjectivity (position, biases, history) of the investigator, and the subjectivity (specificities, self-presentation, history) of the investigated. Inquiry becomes at once self-critical and dialogic."

13. Philip J. Davis and Reuben Hersh, *The Mathematical Experience* (Boston: Houghton Mifflin, 1982).

14. Fred Alan Wolf, *Taking the Quantum Leap: The New Physics for Non Scientists* (San Francisco: Harper & Row, 1981), 6; and *Parallel Universes: The Search for Other Worlds* (New York: Simon and Schuster, 1988). See also David Bohm, "Imagination, Fancy, Insight and Reason in the Process of Thought," in *Evolution of Consciousness, Studies in Polarity*, ed. Shirley Sugerman (Middletown, Conn.: Wesleyan University Press, 1976), 51–68.

15. John Archibald Wheeler, "The Universe as Home for Man," *American Scientist* 62 (November 1974): 689.

16. Maurice Merleau-Ponty, *Phénoméologie de la Perception* (1945), English trans. *Phenomenology of Perception* (New York: Humanities Press, 1962); Merleau-Ponty, *La Structure du Comportement* (1941), English trans. *The Structure of Behavior* (Boston: Beacon Press, 1963); Merleau-Ponty, *Sens et Non-sens* (1948), English trans. *Sense and Nonsense* (Evanston, Ill.: Northwestern University Press, 1964).

17. Nancey C. Murphy, "Does Prayer Make a Difference?" in *Cosmos as Creation: Theology and Science in Consonance*, ed. Ted Peters (Nashville: Abingdon Press, 1989), 244.

18. Dennis Overbye, "Who's Afraid of the Big Bad Bang," *Time*, 26 April 1993, 74.

19. Lewis Wolpert, *The Unnatural Nature of Science* (Cambridge, Mass.: Harvard University Press, 1993). See esp. chap. 2: "Technology Is Not Science," 25–34.

20. Bryan Appleyard, *Understanding the Present: Science and the Soul of Modern Man* (New York: Doubleday, 1992), xvi.

21. Donald A. Norman, *Things That Make Us Smart: Defending Human Attributes in the Age of the Machine* (Reading, Mass.: Addison-Wesley Publishing Co., 1993),

esp. the summary statement on 250. See also Alastair C. MacIntyre, *Whose Justice? Which Rationality?* (Notre Dame, Ind.: University of Notre Dame Press, 1988). For the ethics of "objective" viewpoints and the consequences of the split between knowledge and values, something which he calls "emotivism," see Alastair C. MacIntyre, *After Virtue: A Study in Moral Theory,* 2d ed. (Notre Dame, Ind.: University of Notre Dame Press, 1984), 11–14, 16–35.

22. The Union of Concerned Scientists has issued a similar declaration. See Carl Sagan, "Preserving and Cherishing the Earth: An Appeal for Joint Commitment in Science and Religion," *American Journal of Physics* 58 (1990): 615, 617.

23. Mary Midgley, *Science as Salvation: A Modern Myth and Its Meaning* (New York: Routledge, 1992).

24. John Lukacs, *Confessions of an Original Sinner* (New York: Ticknor & Fields, 1990), 52. Philosopher Hilary Putnam writes that "the deep systemic root of the [objectivist] disease, I want to suggest, lies in the notion of an 'intrinsic' property, a property something has 'in itself,' apart from any contribution made by language or the mind." Putnam, *The Many Faces of Realism: The Paul Carus Lectures* (LaSalle, Ill.: Open Court, 1987), 8.

25. See Rodney Brooks' *Intelligence without Reason* (Cambridge, Mass.: Massachusetts Institute of Technology Artificial Intelligence Laboratory, 1991). In Francisco J. Varela's words, "I am claiming that information—together with all of its closely related notions—has to be reinterpreted as codependent or constructive, in contradistinction to representational or instructive. This means, in other words, a shift from questions about *semantic* correspondence to questions about *structural* patterns." See his *Principles of*

Biological Autonomy (New York: North Holland, 1979), xv. Neni Panourgiá's *Fragments of Death, Fables of Identity: An Athenian Anthropography* (Madison: University of Wisconsin Press, 1995) pioneers a new kind of anthropologist, the "communicative agent," which takes participant observation to the highest level and farthest limits, xxii.

26. The phrase "human informavores" is that of psychologist George A. Miller, "Informavores," in *The Study of Information: Interdisciplinary Messages*, ed. Fritz Machlup and Una Mansfield (New York: John Wiley, 1984), 111–13.

27. Evelyn Fox Keller, *A Feeling for the Organism: The Life and Work of Barbara McClintock* (San Francisco: W. H. Freeman, 1983), 203.

28. Humberto R. Maturana and Francisco J. Varela, *The Tree of Knowledge: The Biological Roots of Human Understanding* (Boston: New Science Library, 1987), 9, 23: "We do not see the 'space' of the world; we live our field of vision. We do not see the 'colors' of the world; we live our chromatic space" (23).

29. Francisco J. Varela, *Principles of Biological Autonomy*, 276.

30. Georges Florovsky, "The Predicament of the Christian Historian," *Religion and Culture: Essays in Honor of Paul Tillich*, ed. Walter Leibrecht (New York: Harper, 1959), 144. Florovsky makes these remarks while reflecting on the rejection of radical empiricism by the French historian Marc Bloch.

31. This antirationalism first sprouted in the 1960s counterculture and flowers profusely in the New Age movement.

32. Francisco J. Varela, Evan Thompson, Eleanor Rosch, *The Embodied Mind: Cognitive Science and Human Experience* (Cambridge, Mass.: MIT Press, 1991), 4.

33. John Ralston Saul's *Voltaire's Bastards: The Dictatorship of Reason in the West* (New York: Free Press, 1992) argues that reason is nothing more than an intellectual tool, not a virtue in and of itself. He uses the "perfectly rational" holocaust as a case study of how blind reason can create nightmare scenarios (74).

34. Quoted in Ted Peters, "Cosmos as Creation," in *Cosmos as Creation: Theology and Science in Consonance*, ed. Ted Peters (Nashville: Abingdon Press, 1989), 46.

35. Pierre Babin and Mercedes Iannone, *The New Era in Religious Communication* (Minneapolis: Fortress Press, 1991), 111.

36. See Varela, et. al., *The Embodied Mind*, 217–19.

37. Nancey C. Murphy, "Does Prayer Make a Difference?" 245. The Forsyth quote is taken from P. T. Forsyth, *The Soul of Prayer* (London: Independent Press, 1954), 90, where he explains: "It is His will, then, that we should pray against what seems His will" (91).

38. In fact, political philosopher Isaiah Berlin's "master key" to understanding eighteenth-century pioneer ethnologist and cultural historian Giambattista Vico adumbrates this E-P-I-C methodology in his famous distinction between two kinds of knowledge: *verum* or *certum*. In *verum*, knowledge is from the outside (in Vico's case, the physical sciences). In *certum*, knowledge is from the inside (especially mathematics and history). See Isaiah Berlin, *Vico and Herder: Two Studies in the History of Ideas* (New York: Viking Press, 1976), 99–114.

39. I am using here the Heideggerian sense of truth as unconcealment (*aletheia*).

40. This figure excludes the 9.3 million business visitors to Washington. See Graham T. T. Molitor's speech "The Next 1000 Years: The 'Big Five,' Engines of Economic Growth," delivered to the World Future Society, Frontiers of the 21st Century, Washington, D.C., 30 July 1999, *Vital Speeches of the Day*, 1 September 1999, 675.

41. Erwin McManus, "Taking on Postmodernism," *Religious Herald*, 4 February 1999, 1–2.

42. Tom Wolfe, *The Electric Kool Aid Acid Test* (New York: Bantam Books, 1969), 129.

✝ ✝ ✝

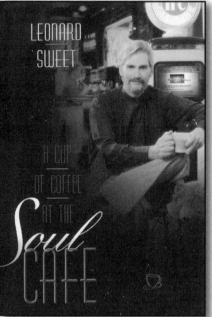